Mourinho Matters

'Football, like other modern sports, is a sublimation of war – fans follow their teams into battle every week, but nobody will actually be killed or maimed.

Mourinho undoubtedly has his devoted followers: first the players in his team, then the many thousands of fans who support that team. He has enjoyed great success in leading his teams to victory, ensuring the devotion of his followers. The crucial test of his charismatic leadership comes when he endures failure.'

John Potts
Professor of Media
Macquarie University

Acknowledgements

To Susan who contributed so much from her professional insights into leadership and her encyclopaedic knowledge of football both from the terraces and the boardrooms of the game.

To Professor John Potts whose knowledge of the charismatic process is unparalleled. His generous contribution in the forward to this book was written uncomplainingly and under time pressure after the news broke of José's departure from Chelsea in November 2015.

To Paul and Conor for invaluable contributions and insights into the delights and agonies of the faithful supporter.

To my students who have taught me so much about football, including Vincent who wisely ignored my advice to follow a career at EUFA after his playing days.

To fans on the terraces whose wit, passion and knowledge of the game create in me a mix of awe, respect and at times despair.

Contents

Forward: by Professor John Potts

Nobody who follows football or watches contemporary media could doubt that José Mourinho is a charismatic leader. The definition of charisma is: *a special innate quality that sets certain individuals apart and draws others to them.*

In case there is any doubt, Mourinho has helpfully named himself 'The Special One'. In press conferences and media appearances, he makes it clear that he is set apart from other football managers and media celebrities: there is something extraordinary about him.

One of Tudor Rickards' achievements in this book is to focus on Mourinho's masterful media appearances, in which he cultivates his 'special' persona.

But a leader's charisma is based primarily on success. When the sociologist Max Weber developed his theory of the charismatic leader in the early twentieth century, he had in mind warrior-leaders, war heroes, leaders in the hunt, or religious leaders such as prophets, shamans or magicians. For each of these early leaders, success was the basis of their leadership. Success in battle, or in healing, or in causing seemingly supernatural events, ensured that the leader maintained a following of loyal supporters. The charisma of the leader allows him (Weber's examples are almost all male) to galvanise his following through electrifying speeches, but if success dries up, so too does the following.

Weber did not live long enough to apply his idea of the charismatic leader to entertainers, or celebrities. But a highly successful football manager such as Mourinho is a strong candidate for being treated as a Weberian charismatic leader within the fields of sport and entertainment.

Football, like other modern sports, is a sublimation of war – fans follow their teams into battle every week, but nobody will actually be killed or maimed. Mourinho undoubtedly has his devoted followers: first the players in his team, then the many thousands of fans who support that team. He has enjoyed great success in leading his teams to victory, ensuring the devotion of his followers. The crucial test of his charismatic leadership comes when he endures failure – and here again Tudor Rickards closely follows Mourinho's fortunes when he suffers failure at Chelsea.

Ultimately, it should be obvious that there is something irrational about charisma. A football team's success cannot rationally be attributed to one person. Success is due to the efforts of the players, guided by their manager; it is equally due to the administration of the club and how much money its owners can spend on players.

But the belief persists that one man – a 'Special One' – is responsible for a team's achievements. No-one has embodied this belief more prominently than José Mourinho, who has exerted a mighty act of will in maintaining the idea that a team's success can be attributed to his special abilities.

How does he do this? Tudor Rickards traces his methods, his successes and failures, in this engrossing book.

Preface

When my students offer examples of outstanding sporting leaders, José Mourinho is invariably mentioned. When I ask what makes him so remarkable, one of the first suggestions is his charismatic personality.

This takes us nicely into questions raised during classroom discussions about the still mysterious subject of charisma:

What is it?
Who has it?
How can you get more of it?

Even so, José would have remained just one among my ever-increasing collection of charismatic leaders if it had it not been for a sudden and unexpected turn of events in the early months of the 2015-16 football season in England.

Premier League football champions Chelsea, managed by José Mourinho start losing game after game. To the astonishment of fans and pundits alike, the team plummet towards the relegation zone. No immediate League Championship team has ever performed as badly as this before at the start of the following season. News stories appear explaining what is happening.

One theory is that José had lost it big time. He has lost the confidence of Chelsea's wealthy and ambitious owner Roman Abramovich. He has lost the support of the legions of sports journalists who had previously been writing admiringly about him.

And worst of all, he has '*lost the dressing room*', that mysterious closed world in which the trust of players in their leaders is made or destroyed.

Tales from the dressing room have to be assessed very carefully. They are difficult to authenticate and are often leaked via disillusioned players or from secondary sources. Nevertheless, something very interesting was happening at Chelsea.

As I followed the daily news accounts, I could see a dramatic tale unfolding of a leader who was unable to change the downturn in fortune to his career and reputation.

By November 2015, it seemed likely that the drama was approaching a spectacular conclusion. I began to wonder if it would be possible to understand charisma by a closer examination of the Mourinho case, together with materials I had written about in my earlier work on leadership and charisma. I hoped so, and rearranged my writing schedules accordingly. I collected together a series of posts which I wrote initially for leadership students over the period 2008-2015 and which appeared in the blog Leaders We Deserve.

Each of these posts examined a current news story and presented it to encourage readers to search for relevance in their own leadership experiences. These have been updated here, with the benefits of hindsight, as postscripts, leaving the original content intact beyond a minimum of changes to improve the clarity of the material.

I began a more careful monitoring of the emerging stories for José's last tumultuous months at Chelsea. The ones which seemed the most significant I wrote up in the same informal style as the existing Leaders We Deserve cases.

I wanted to write *Mourinho Matters* for an audience interested in football and in the fascinating story of José Mourinho. To this end I have left the main body of the text without the visible signs of scholarship such as footnotes and reference sources. Readers are able to treat the book as an interesting and enjoyable (I hope) story. The content is a mix of descriptions of factual events with some personal observations. I have also included book reviews on topics such as charismatic leadership, and the theory of football tactics. Anyone wanting to study Mourinho Matters more carefully, for research or as part of a leadership curriculum, will be able to do so, by drawing on the references sources and index supplied. The original Leaders We Deserve posts published on-line used web-based sources. I have retained the references in that format. If you chose to study using a web-based approach, I suggest that you also use a standard printed textbook in support of your on-line work. For this, I recommend *A History of Charisma* by John Potts as suitable for deeper studies of charisma, and my textbook *Dilemmas of Leadership* for contemporary and historic leadership theories which are to be found in business, sport and political writings.

Introduction

At the start of the 2015-16 Premier League season in England, in the unseasonable month of July, Chelsea football club was widely expected to be about to have another successful year as it set out to defend its title as league champions under its charismatic manager José Mourinho

Before the league season was underway, there was a competitive game which produced an unexpected result. As league champions, Chelsea played the winners of the FA Cup in the Community Shield competition held annually between the Premier League and FA Cup champions. Their opponents were Arsenal. Chelsea lost narrowly, getting their new season off to a poor start. One of the talking points afterwards was that the result was a success for Arsène Wenger, the Arsenal Manager. his first victory over José Mourinho in fourteen attempts in various competitions.

As July advanced into August, various unpleasant records were being broken. League matches were lost often against modest opposition.

In José Mourinho's 200th Premier League match, Chelsea's 1–2 defeat to Crystal Palace was only José's second home defeat at Stamford Bridge in his long and illustrious Chelsea career.

Chelsea were eight points behind leaders Manchester City at the end of August and were languishing 13th in the premiership league table. Critics enjoyed the unusual reversal in the customary state of footballing affairs.

By September, their poor form was being seen increasingly as more than a temporary blip. At the month's end, Chelsea were 15th in the Premiership table.

October saw a continuation of Chelsea's depressing run of results. By the end of the month, they remained deeply embedded at the wrong end of the league table. By November, their chances of retaining their Premier League Champions' title had all but vanished. Mourinho's prospects of remaining manager were also being discussed on the terraces and by football pundits. Chelsea's miserable campaign continued with a defeat at West Ham, during which both managers were banished from the touchlines.

The BBC's weekend *Match of the Day* programme began to turn themselves into *Loss of the Day*. Chelsea's game was made the first item on the show, which in the past selected the most exciting match of the day, or the one involving the battle for leading positions in the Premiership league tables.

To understand what might be happening, we have to go back into the turbulent career of José Mourinho.

Back to his triumphant days as a young manager breaking records with Porto in his native Portugal. Then to his time at Chelsea then as European Champions Cup winner with Inter Milan, and his battles at Real Madrid against an all-conquering Barcelona team. before returning to Chelsea.

Mourinho Matters begins with his early year of success, his *annus mirabilis*. It ends with his greatest period of managerial crisis. I could not help seeing this as his year of misery, his *annus horribilis*.

Early Days

Long before I started writing about him, José Mário dos Santos Félix Mourinho was a young Portuguese schoolboy growing up in comfortable home surroundings, intent on becoming a professional footballer. His father, José Félix Mourinho, was a goalkeeper, and there can be little doubt that the competitive José would have wanted to outperform the father by becoming a top international player.

José junior was also smart enough to realise quickly that his talents were more suited to coaching than to playing the beautiful game.

He avidly learned the principles of sports science at the Technical university of Lisbon, and was also gifted linguistically. These talents, plus a capacity for hard work would have been enough for success even without that other favourable factor of a lucky break.

That came with the arrival in Portugal of the great England coach and former international Bobby Robson who was looking for a local coach who could act as an interpreter. Bobby was as poor at languages as he was gifted as a coach. José was on his way. José fitted the bill perfectly, sharing in Robson's achievements.

With Robson as mentor, he moved from Sporting Lisbon with coaching and interpreting duties. Their time there was hugely successful, putting in place a structure at the club which persisted after Robson moved on.

In 1996 Robson accepted the plum job of managing Barcelona. He again negotiated for his young assistant to join him there. This was to be one of the formative periods in José's football education. Later, his admiration was soured by a failure to be appointed chief coach at the club.

Robson's dazzling results at Barça were marred by his increasing ill-health, and he returned to England leaving José to pursue his football education under another brilliant manager Louis van Gaal.

Years later, van Gaal was to find himself attempting to revive the fortunes of Manchester United at the time when José was manager during his second period at Chelsea.

José returned to Porto in early 2002, this time as head coach. It was the perfect appointment. Mourinho already had a deep knowledge of the club and its players from his time there with Bobby Robson. Now he could have more control adding more of his own ideas to those he had learned from Robson and more briefly from van Gaal

In 2003 he won three trophies with Porto, the Primeira Liga, Taça de Portugal, and UEFA Cup in 2003. In the next season, won the highest honour in European club football, the UEFA Champions League.

With a little chronological licence, I have nominated the period spanning parts of two seasons his annus mirabilis.

Statistics alone do not capture the extraordinary self-confidence displayed by José from his early days in the public limelight. I can't resist sharing one anecdote which sums this up for me. When asked in a Radio interview what he believed God thought about him, José replied:

'He must really think I'm a great guy. He must think that, because otherwise He would not have given me so much. I have a great family. I work in a place where I've always dreamt of working. He has helped me out so much that He must have a very high opinion of me.'

If God has a pretty high opinion of José, why shouldn't José have a pretty high opinion of himself as well?

Annus Mirabilis

May 25 2004

These previously unpublished notes were originally written at the time Porto with Mourinho as manager won the much coveted European Champions League trophy.

Looking back at the start of José's career, I am reminded of the term Annus mirabilis, the year of wonders, which was the title of a poem of the same name written over four centuries earlier.

In 1666 a great fire tore through the wooden entrails of the city of London. In its wake, a dazed nation began the rebuilding from the charred, remains. A year later, John Dryden wrote a patriotic poem celebrating the resilience of the nation in peace and in war. He called it *Annus mirabilis*, the year of wonders. Dryden assumed that readers would know that the annus mirabilis was a time of regained confidence after the truly horrible year of the great fire.

Four centuries later Queen Elizabeth II referred to her family's annus horribilis after personal tragedies capped with a fire at Windsor Castle.

José's annus mirabilis came early in his career in the football season, and his annus horribilis, as we will see, came much later.

In 2003-3 a young and relatively inexperienced coach takes Porto, an unfancied Portuguese club, to the summit of European football season by winning the Champions League trophy.

The official website of EUFA headlines the achievement as 'Porto pull off biggest surprise'.

The victory completes a notable treble. He has already won Portugal's Liga Sagres Championship and the national cup competition.

A technical study of football teams for the decade 2000-2009.later nominates Mourinho's Porto side fourth in a list of the top ten teams. The article points out that Mourinho started as an untested manager with a group of relatively unknown players drawn from the obscurity of unfashionable clubs in Portugal's Liga Sagres.

José's career has started in a style that is already making him attractive to the top clubs in Europe ambitious to win the prestigious European Cup competition for themselves. How has he reinvented Porto into the best team not just in Portugal, but arguably the best in Europe in less than a year?

Three factors are coming together to stunning effect. First of all, José has identified relatively unknown players of great potential. Secondly, the team plays with a commitment and intensity which suggests he has a top manager's ability to motivate players consistently. His motivational powers are seen repeatedly in the intensity of his touchline performances, his anguish at any player's violation of his rehearsed plans, his triumphal celebrations at a goal scored from a well-executed move. And thirdly, José is applying a depth of thinking and meticulous planning to the job of managing the club.

The talent he recognizes at Porto includes two full backs, Nuno Valente from Leiria, and Paolo Ferreira from Vitoria de Setubal. They have great speed and physical strength. He coaches them to launch speedy attacks which terrified opposing defenders.

The wing attacks are protected by a protective defensive midfield structure (three 'holding midfielders', as football commentators like to say). His skills at establishing effective defensive systems are to remain important throughout his career.

According to the website Zonal Marking, the structure introduced at Porto by Mourinho is not particularly innovative.

'However, they were without question the most well-drilled club side [on the list of teams of the decade]. The defensive line was incredibly effective at catching opposition forwards offside, often playing high up the pitch and using a frankly aggressive offside trap that continued to bamboozle opposition forwards. The midfield worked as a unit rather than a collection of individuals, and Mourinho used different forwards according to the opposition at hand.'

This description shows that José is first recognised for qualities which are not particularly associated with a charismatic leader. In Business School speak, I see them as illustrating the effective use of the principles of situational leadership.

For example, he selects teams according to his analysis of each situation he faces, assessing the strengths and weaknesses of his own players and deploys them as the situation demands.

According to this theory, as a team becomes more mature, the leader has to modify his or her approach. In everyday terms, this requires knowing when a tough controlling approach is called for, and when an 'arms round the shoulder' way is better. Tightly controlled leadership to reinforce desired patters of play has to give way to more supportive mentoring or coaching approaches.

The general approach is often described as an '*it all depends*' theory. It is one thing to recognise flexibility as an important leadership trait. However, as one professional leadership coach put it 'it all depends, but on what?'

Postscript:

Without the benefits of hindsight, we cannot infer what is particularly special about José's style. We will need more evidence before understanding the factors contributing to José's remarkably rise to prominence as a top football coach.

Understanding José's Overnight Success

How did José succeed so brilliantly and quickly towards the start of his managerial career at Porto?

As José attracted media attention he is widely regarded as having a highly charismatic leadership style. At first, however, as I suggested, his success may have been seen not so much as due to special level of skills, but high levels of results applying necessary basic skills recognised as important in all football managers including dedication, hard work, motivation, and a capacity to develop and execute strategic plans in a flexible way.

In other words, he was seen not as a person with special skills, but as a person with the same skills as those to be found among less successful managers, but developed in him to a higher degree.

I would add to that his head start from a favourable home environment together with personal qualities including motivation to succeed, and capacity to learn quickly from his mentors.

José had been immersed in a footballing culture from his childhood. He had a voracious appetite for learning everything he could about the game. As a student of sports science he studied and discussed the latest ideas about football tactics which were emerging in international competitions.

Before taking up his first managerial post, he had absorbed the ideas of two brilliant football mentors, Bobby Robson and then Louis van Gaal. José 's own approach was not an imitation of either, but one which drew selectively on what we learned from each of them.

Robson was an intuitive manager. Mourinho later reflected that Bobby had concentrated on attacking formations and ideas, leaving his young assistant to develop defensive plans.

Van Gaal was and still remains a more conceptual thinker than Robson. He reflects thinks deeply and obsessively about players, as well as the nature of developing them and the importance of football strategy and formations. He later was to describe his approach as a coherent philosophy which can only be learned over an extended period of time in discussion with him. Mourinho has a similar obsessional belief in detailed planning.

In the space of a year, José is propelled from apprentice to a position as someone rated as a leading manager in Europe.

But this overnight success story is illusory. It is rather like that of the actor who bursts into public consciousness to become lan overnight sensation.

The reality is that the actor, just like José, had put in years of training which contributed to the sudden emergence of a star when the opportunity presents itself. Unexpected success is closer to overnight recognition than it is to overnight development of super powers.

There is a lively debate continuing about the nature of exceptional talent. A major contribution has come from the brilliant writings of the social commentator Malcolm Gladwell, and in particular his book Outliers.

Gladwell suggests that outstanding achievers put in thousands of hours of motivated work before their talent is developed and appears effortless. There are many anecdotal accounts from sport to back up his idea. There is an obsessive compulsion and motivation from an early age. Natural talent combines with motivation and opportunity (which is helped along by mentors or parental encouragement).

The debate is mainly over how much natural talent (or maybe unnatural talent) goes into the production of an exceptional performer. Did Serena and Venus Williams have a natural talent that was waiting to be released, or might there be hundreds of potential Wimbledon winners capable of making it with the right training and motivation?

As might be expected, there are supporters of a 'nothing special' view who point to the way a cluster of champions can be produced and developed into a winning team.

The table tennis champion and sports journalist Mathew Syad, in his book Bounce, supports Gladwell's *ten thousand hours* hypothesis and argues the case for the 'nothing special' school of thought. He draws on his own experience in which a school teacher with access to a secure training hall produced a remarkable number of top players from one local school.

The debate is a more specific version of the nature or nurture one. The evidence suggests that natural ability is necessary but not sufficient for success as a football manager, an athlete or a business tycoon. Dedication, and chance opportunities are also nrequired. Little wonder that Napoleon is reported as saying he had a preference or 'lucky' Generals in combat. Returning to José, we might see his success as drawing on factors involving motive, means and opportunities.

So where does his much-reported charisma come into the story? To answer that we have to look briefly at the nature and history of charismatic leadership. In this book, as John Potts indicates in his Forward, the charismatic leader appears to possess 'a special innate quality that sets certain individuals apart and draws others to them'.

When exceptional success occurs, it attributed not just to the 'ordinary' skills of planning, but to that innate quality which cannot be explained without recourse to a mysterious giftedness.

The influential work of sociologist Max Weber in the early twentieth century suggested that in early primitive societies, 'warrior-leaders, war heroes, leaders in the hunt, or religious leaders such as prophets, shamans or magicians' obtained their status through success in battle, or in healing, or in causing seemingly supernatural events, ensured that the leader maintained a following of loyal supporters. A highly successful football manager such as Mourinho is a strong candidate for being considered charismatic. 'Football, like other modern sports, is a sublimation of war – fans follow their teams into battle every week, but nobody will actually be killed or maimed. Mourinho undoubtedly has his devoted followers: first the players in his team, then the many thousands of fans who support that team. He has enjoyed great success in leading his teams to victory, ensuring the devotion of his followers. The crucial test of his charismatic leadership comes when he endures failure.'

José, like the ancient shamans, was to develop similar skills at beguiling an audience with his 'spell-binding' accounts of his glorious victories, and promises of future success.

John Potts also warns of the frequent fate of the charismatic leader. When success disappears, charisma fades too. An *annus mirabilis* begins a story which may end in bitter disappointment, an *annus horribilis*.

But for the moment, José is on a winning streak. He is about to join Chelsea, one of the wealthiest football clubs in the world.

The Tinkerman

May 31 2004

In May 2004, Claudio Ranieri was coach of Chelsea football club. His appointment ended with the arrival of José Mourinho, fresh from his triumphs at Porto. Claudio was to figure in our story later at several crucial times in his and José's career paths

Claudio Ranieri is a rare individual among those to be found in the top reaches of football management. He exudes amiability towards the world, combined with passion towards the game from the touch line.

He arrived in England in 2000 to coach Chelsea. In a short period of time, Ranieri produced results. He took the club to runner-up in the Premiership, its best ever position. To this he added a semi-final appearance of the European Cup in the year Mourinho's Porto emerged as winning finalists.

Only the most churlish fans of the 'runners up are losers' mentality complained. Mostly, the Chelsea supporters were delighted with their rather idiosyncratic manager. They were even able to enjoy Claudio's relentless search for the best team, and his tinkering with starting positions which earned him his reputation as 'the Tinkerman' His amiable press conferences added to his popularity.

Then, unexpectedly, in 2003, Chelsea was acquired by the Multi Billionaire Roman Abramovich. The most radical change in fortunes in the Club's history was about to begin.

From the outset, it was clear that Abramovich''s intention was to turn Chelsea Football Club into European champions and to consolidate their future as a global force in world football. He quickly set out to buy the best players, pay the best wages, and, no secret, hire the best coaches that his Russian petrodollars could buy.

Ranieri was seen as a temporary appointment. An attempt was first made to lure Sven-Goran Ericsson to Chelsea away from his position as coach to England's national team. When that proved unsuccessful, attention turned to Mourinho who was adding to his reputation as a top manager with the European successes he achieved at Porto.

Claudio Ranieri was shrewd enough to know that his days as Manager at Chelsea were numbered. In his biography, Ranieri tells how, as speculation was growing, he and the Chelsea squad were about to take a short break from training. Owner and coach were chatting, privately and amiably.

"When will the players be back in training?" the owner asked. I can picture the twinkle in Ranieri's eye as he replied "When the new coach says so". Both men looked at each other, and burst into laughter.

Claudio's prediction about his departure quickly came about. José Mourinho's first appointment at Chelsea was about to begin.

Chelsea's Magical Mystery Tour

August 15 2004

What a dawn it was. With scarcely a bump in the road, José Mourinho arrived fresh from his startling successes in Porto. He took charge of Chelsea's shiny new footballing machine with instructions to drive it on towards the dream future planned for it by its wealthy owner.

Fans, still recovering rather like jackpot winners, increasingly realized they were to take part in a magical mystery tour, unhampered by mundane issues such as financial restrictions. But it was not so much *Penny Lane*, rather *Baby, You're a Rich Man Now*.

José and Roman had arrived. For the fans, it was not just jam today and jam tomorrow. It was Caviar and Champagne today, and ever after.

Arsenal, Manchester United, even Real Madrid and Barcelona, stared apprehensively at the potential threat from the Stamford Bridge club.

The Chelsea fans gave little thought that anything could go wrong ever again. No one much paid attention to the fact that José was still quite an inexperienced manager in a hurry.

José had begun his managerial career only four years earlier, at Sporting Lisbon The appointment there owed much to his English mentor Bobby Robson. A year later he was at União de Leiria, central Portugal, a little club which was swept forward briefly before José moved back to Sporting Lisbon and then Porto in his annus mirabilis.

When he arrived in Chelsea in 2004, it was his fourth club in four years. But that breath-taking journey was surely now over. The Special One had found a special club. As he would repeat in countless spell-binding press conferences, this was true love, never to be broken.

In his first game as manager, Chelsea playing at home faced Manchester United, the club that was dominating the football scene in England. Its wily manager Alex Ferguson, (later Sir

Alex) was already establishing his reputation as one of the greatest football managers of all time.

In the five years that had passed since José started his footballing career, Manchester United had won a cluster of league championships and had become the first team to win the Premier League, FA Cup and the European Champions League in the same season.

José was fond of reminding the press of his own similar 'treble' success during his annus mirabilis at Porto, although competition in Portugal to win its league and cup was weaker than was experienced by Ferguson at Manchester United.

Fifteen minutes into José's first game as manager, his newly strengthened team burst through the Manchester United defences and scored.

Chelsea defended their precious one goal lead with a tenacity that was to become one of the strengths of Mourinho's teams. José was on his way to his first win as the Blues boss.

Chelsea's magical mystery tour had begun.

Sweet Scent of Victory or Low-hanging Fruit?

April 30 2005

It all went so well at first. In José's first season. Chelsea, with its coterie of top players brought in with Abramovich's buying power began to sweep all before them.

Towards the start of his first season at Chelsea in August 2004, José had begun one of those exercises in prediction and crystal-ball gazing that endeared him to the media.

He pronounced that from his study of the fixture list, he could tell that the match against Bolton Wanderers towards the end of the season would be where and when Chelsea would win their first ever Premier league championship.

Note to students of leadership: Examine how mystics and magicians through the ages achieve their results. [Hint: Consider José's prediction at the start of the season for the importance of the game against Bolton at the end. Consider how the prophets tend to retain the trust of their followers when a prediction turns out to be wrong.]

By the time that the Bolton match arrived, Chelsea seemed to closing in on the Premiership, and were about to fulfil José 's.

Chelsea had lost only one game in the league throughout the season. Its obsessively planned defensive system had conceded only thirteen goals throughout. John Terryleader of the defence, was tipped to be voted Chelsea's player of the year.

The sweet scent of victory was in the air for the Chelsea fans who travelled to Bolton's neat little Reebok stadium

Chelsea were not just close to their first league championship. They were still in the Champions League at the knockout stage. Another treble was a possibility for José. This time he could not be accused of victories against modest opposition as might have been the case in Portugal. Now he was triumphing against Premier league opponents such as the mighty Manchester United managed by the legendary Alex Ferguson.

Awaiting them at Bolton was a team managed by the wily campaigner 'Big Sam' Allardyce, epitome of a gritty northerner, and often compared in style and looks to the burly police chief Andy Dalziel played in the TV series by Warren Clarke.

Sam had drilled his team to play in his own dour but resilient fashion. Chelsea could expect no easy capitulation. Bolton had grabbed a point for a hard earned draw at Stamford Bridge in the reverse fixture in November. They were themselves contenders for an unusual top-six finish through teamwork plus the skill of Gary Speed and the muscular attacking force of striker Kevin Davies.

Kevin struck an early if accidental blow on John Terry who ended the first half with a fast developing eye injury that might have stopped the contest if it had been in a boxing match. Terry typically led the team out after the interval. That could edge it in the voting for Chelsea's man of the season.

It was left to Frank Lampard, another of Chelsea's top performers, to break the deadlock. As one of Chelsea's attacks built up, he cut in from midfield as he had been doing all season (bet you warned them about that, Sam) and scored a precise goal.

Now Bolton had to attack, and as they did so they were picked off. Lampard found his path to goal even less well-defended, and he moved forward and swerved around the helpless goalkeeper to score again.

Cue delirious outburst from the Chelsea fans. A friend watching the match recalled to me later how José celebrated the goal by dashing ecstatically along the touchline, arms upraised, black long-coat flapping. His prophecy had come true. José had begun to deliver the trophies that had eluded Chelsea in over a century of competitive football.

This was to be a highlight of Mourinho's first season with Chelsea. The team was not able to deliver up to José his second European Championship to go with his victory with Porto the previous season. That was to go to another Premiership side. But it was not Manchester United, but Liverpool, managed by Rafa Benitez, who beat AC Milan in the final.

Liverpool had dominated in Europe in the 1980s, but had since witnessed Manchester United replaced them as the strongest team in the Premiership.

In 2005 Liverpool had finished fourth in the Premiership which would have prevented them qualifying for the competition the following year. Their comeback from 3-0 down at half time against Milan gave them their fifth European Champions trophy. The match became known as the Miracle of Istanbul, and added to the club's outstanding performances in European championships.

In one of those coincidences, Liverpool's victory came after a miss in the penalty shoot-out by Andriy Shevchenko. Soon afterwards, Abramovich brought Shevchenko to Chelsea. He was to become part of a dispute between the owner and Mourinho regarding the players needed to strengthen the squad.

The Chelsea fans celebrated a successful season. This was not the time to suggest that the result had been achieved with a team mostly built by the departing Tinkerman Claudio Ranieri. However, the Mourinho magic was not working as well on football journalists trained to detect overblown claims. The gap between Chelsea and the top European teams did not close as quickly as was expected on José's arrival. The possibility began to be raised in the press that the early victory might have been gained through harvesting low hanging fruit and that there were to be far tougher challenges ahead.

Postscript:

John Terry was to receive widespread recognition for his defensive play in Chelsea's resurgence. He went on to become one of José 's greatest players throughout their times together at Chelsea. He was a dominant influence in the 2004-5 season when Chelsea's Premier League title was built on an astonishing defensive record. The season ended with Chelsea's results standing at: Played 38, Wins 29, Draws 8, losses 1, Goals for 72, Goals against 15, Points 95.

The success of the 2004-5 side was put down to the defensive leadership of youthful JohnTerry, with Didier Drogba as a ballistic missile of a forward, supported by Frank Lampard, with Claude Makelele, a dominant midfield defender.

Terry contributed eight valuable goals out of defence. Among the awards he won that season was Player of the Year, voted by his fellow professionals. No Chelsea player had won the award before, since its inception in the season 1972-3. It was to be more than a decade before another Chelsea player won the award, Eden Hazard in the 2014-5 season.

As we will see, both Hazard and Terry were to play important parts in the final months of Mourinho's second period at Chelsea, a decade later.

Momentum shifts at Stamford Bridge and Adelaide

December 27 2006

The following year, when champions Chelsea ran out at Stamford Bridge for the Boxing Day fixture against Reading, the match could be seen as particularly influenced by momentum swings. A similar interpretation could be placed on the humiliation of England Cricket team by Australia in the Boxing Day test in faraway Adelaide.

The term 'momentum' is being used frequently to describe the ebb and flow of sporting encounters. For example, Chelsea had been seen as a team that had lost ground in comparison to its performance in José's first year. This was explained as losing momentum since the loss of goalkeeper Petr Cech, a key player.

Nevertheless, José's watertight defensive set ups still made Chelsea one of the most difficult teams to beat on their home ground.

In the Boxing Day game at Stanford Bridge, Chelsea took the lead against relegation candidates Reading. The away team battled back and levelled the game. Then Chelsea regrouped and regained the lead. Just as the natural order of things seemed to have been restored, Reading scored a last minute equalizer.

The Reading coach Steve Coppell talked about the momentum swings in the match:

"We had a defined game plan and the players stuck resolutely to that. I think 1-0 down is a precarious position to be in, but we really pushed on. There was a real determination in the dressing room. The players were very positive and the momentum was with us for the second half. Once we got back in I thought we might have gone on to win the game. We had a bit of fortune for the second goal. We are pleased with the point. We haven't played well recently."

But had there been a clear swing of momentum? Let's differentiate between physical momentum and psychological momentum. In October, in their previous encounter, the momentum of a Reading defender's physical challenge on Petr Cech had put Chelsea's star goalkeeper out of action until the New Year. That's physical momentum and the consequences of its sudden transference.

The sportswriters are commenting on Chelsea losing momentum to challengers and league table leaders Manchester United. I want to suggest that they are now referring to psychological momentum.

There is a lot of talk in football and other sports about momentum – gaining it, losing it, or retaining it. But just what is momentum? In dynamics, it's the energy possessed by moving objects. It's an important concept for figuring out what happens when cars hit people (on either side of the windscreen). Big fast objects have a lot of momentum, small slow-moving ones a lot less. Momentum at the point of impact helps sport scientists explain golf swings, tennis serves, Grand Prix shunts and a host more consequences of impact incidents.

The physical momentum in a tackle possesses energy which is very rapidly absorbed by a second object. That was what happened and wiped out Petr Cech. It is a quantifiable measure to do with the energy possessed by moving objects and its transference to other objects such as golf balls, or a boxer's (or in Petr Cech's case a footballer's) skull.

If we take another of this week's sporting stories, we see the term being used to refer to psychological momentum.

In Adelaide, a cricket test match was beginning between Australia and England.

For readers unfamiliar with cricket's iconography I should explain that Australia beat England in a historical test-match and won a series of matches or 'tests'. This produced a sacred relic in the physical form of a carbonised piece of wood (part of the primitive device determining the fate of a batsman). The ashes of the device were encased in a small funeral urn in the tradition of an ancient Greek amphora of the sixth century BCE Athenian era. It is about the size of a small modern perfume bottle or of a juvenile gerbil.

Test matches between England and Australia are now contested for The Ashes, the right to retain the sacred urn and its contents to be displayed in the most hallowed shrine of the victorious country.

England had won the previous series in England. However, in the first of what became known as the 'Sackcloth and Ashes' tests all confidence seemed to have drained from England.

In the first over of the series, fast bowler Steve Harmison had a career-wrecking attack of the yips and had to be removed permanently from the attack.

Australia tortured and humiliated the depleted England team for five days. Momentum well and truly swung to the Aussies write the cricket pundits.

Then the Boxing Day test arrives. It started with a great batting performance from England. In the first innings they scored over 500 runs, a near match-winning total.

Momentum was said to have been regained. England had even declared, a psychologically powerful move giving the winning team more time to polish off their already weakened opponents. The declaration did not have the desired effect. Australia, far from being psychologically defeated... replied with an even mightier total.

The journalists start suggesting that the momentum has unexpectedly swung again. The England batsmen would have to survive where they had crumbled on countless occasions before. Australis were about to unleash their most powerful weapon, the guiles of Steve Warne, the greatest spin bowler of his time, and on an aging and unpredictable batting surface.

Kevin Pietersen, England's own unpredictable batting genius was needed to perform heroics. Instead he passed from brilliance to banality with one over-casual waft which cost him his wicket.

Any confidence left in the England camp evaporated into the Adelaide air. Australia had just enough time to hit off the required runs. As a dejected BBC sports correspondent put it:

'No team in history has lost after declaring on a higher total than England's 551-6 batting first in a Test'. Unfortunately, this team did. The sports journalists scribbled scathingly about Pieteren's irresponsible swing of his bat and the subsequent swing of momentum.

Returning to the Chelsea match, the team 'only' manages a draw against newly-promoted Reading. José Mourinho says that his team has a short-term problem. Its defence was severely damaged by the losses of Cech, and more recently to their inspirational captain Terry. Momentum has been lost.

Strictly speaking, a loss of momentum in their bid to retain their title would be reflected in a dip in playing form. They have suffered important injuries. Yet, over the last few weeks, the results have been good enough to retain their lead over all the clubs below them and even reduce the gap between themselves and league-toppers Manchester United.

Even in adversity, they have had players to rescue them from dropping points. They have scored last-minute winners themselves in two recent matches, not a sign of a side that has lost momentum.

I am collecting examples of descriptions of momentum swings, mostly from rugby, football, cricket and tennis matches. I am still looking for convincing evidence that the concept has much predictive power.

Too often it is a form of an elegant tautology, as a commentator or player searches for another way of saying "I didn't see that coming".

Paul Revere Rides again ("The Americans are Coming")

February 6 2007

The arrival of a Russian owner at Chelsea was only one of a series of recent 'invasions' by investors keen to gain control of England's football clubs. When two American businessmen bought Liverpool Football Club in 2007, I started researching the foreign forces acquiring England's Premiership football teams. In patriotic style, I issued a call to arms to alert a slumbering nation.

In *The Midnight Ride of Paul Revere*, Henry Longfellow wrote in fine galloping style about one of the most famed and patriotic actions in the run-up to the American war of independence.

On April 18, 1775, Paul Revere, a Bostonian silversmith by trade, alerted the American militia of the approaching British forces with the rousing cry to arms "The British are coming". This time it is the Americans who are advancing and seizing control of England's Premier football teams.

I want to turn Paul Revere's warning cry on its head to British football fans in the early years of the 21st century that "The Americans are coming" as well as invaders from other parts of the globe.

On 6 February 2007, Liverpool Football Club has passed from the ownership of local entrepreneur David Moores to that of two American businessmen George Gillett and Tom Hicks

The event met with surprisingly little resistance from supporters on Merseyside. In that respect, it was in contrast to the fans' response to another American takeover at Manchester United two years earlier.

When the Glazers, a family of American sporting entrepreneurs had taken over Manchester United Football in 2004, the fans rose up in a display of organized resistance. Their initial reactions were intense suspicion that the move was primarily in the interests of short-term financial manipulation.

The more extreme predictions have not come to pass, and by 2007 the club was experiencing another upsurge of good results on the pitch. Boycotts by disaffected season ticket holders have been rather ineffective, as the enlarged stadium at Old Trafford since the take-over has regularly claimed Premier league record attendances.

But the outcry at MUFC was not replicated in other foreign takeovers of Premier league clubs. At Chelsea FC, fans appreciated the potential of what appeared to be an unlimited budget provided by Russian Billionaire Roman Abramovich.

At Aston Villa, another American sporting entrepreneur, Randy Werner, also met with little opposition from the fans. This might have been in part due to the leadership style of its former owner, Doug Ellis. Despite all his dedicated efforts and investment of a sizable chunk his own fortune, his willingness to fire the coaches he appointed had earned him his nickname of Deadly Doug.

West Ham United also succumbed to an overseas offer, this from Björgólfur Guðmundsson an Icelandic football administrator and retailing entrepreneur. Arsenal FC, one of the elite and revered names of English football, retained its broad governance, but at the cost of moving into a new stadium re-named after its backers, the United Emirates.

The threat of foreign invasion was less acute elsewhere in Europe. Italy's clubs remain beset with a range of legal and political scandals. Such turmoil did not prevent Italy last year winning the greatest prize of all, The World Cup on German soil. Italy's leading football clubs tend to have backers of enormous resources and have not been such an attraction for American sporting entrepreneurs.

Nor have the clubs in Spain, which can boast two of the world's most glamorous and wealthy clubs in Barcelona and Real Madrid. Top teams in Germany and France, while less wealthy, have national structures and business models which make them secure from foreign invasion. Among the European nations, England has been rather open to new ownership. There is an interesting parallel with the openness to foreign ownership of commercial concerns, for example in the automotive industry.

Postscript:

Liverpool's first American owners laater lost control of the club which had run into severe financial difficulties. On 15 October 2010, ownership passed to another American organization, the Fenway Sports Group

Björgólfur Guðmundsson lost his fortune in the 2008 financial crisis. As head of the leading Icelandic bank, Landsbanki, he has been considered one of the major figures in the Country's financial decline. West Ham was later returned to English ownership when it was acquired by 'the two Davids' (David Gold and David Sullivan)

Manchester United supporters continued to fight a dogged campaign against the owners of the club, which seemed to be dropping behind the footballing achievements of Chelsea and its billionaire owner. In 2011, a greater threat to Manchester United's supremacy was to come from a takeover of the less prestigious local team Manchester City.

Dubbed the noisy neighbours by United's legendary manager Sir Alex Ferguson, City was acquired by the Abu Dhabi United Group and became one of the richest football clubs in the world.

In the same year, Paris Saint-Germain (PSG) also found a similarly wealthy owner in Qatar Sports Investments.

But the iron law of economics still applied. 'To them that hath shall it be given.' In England, Chelsea and later Manchester City were eventually to outpace other contenders, in money for the best available players and obtaining most successful international managers.

In contrast, Manchester United was to become seen as in the possession of the relatively modestly endowed family down the road, albeit of noble origins, trying to keep up appearances with their noisy but wealthy and ambitious neighbours.

What José did next

March 7 2007

Chelsea football club won a vital European cup-game against Mourinho's former club Porto after a poor first-half performance. Much of the improvement was attributed to the influence exerted by charismatic coach José Mourinho through his half-time exhortation. This appears to be a case example of a leader's inspiring influence. But is it as simple as all that? Are there lessons others can learn and imitate successfully?

For forty-five minutes, the current champions of the English Premiership played like the underdogs (which they weren't) and almost like the away team (which they also weren't).

The visitors, Porto, cashed in on their superiority through a well-taken goal after fifteen minutes, a lead they held until the half-time.

Coach José Mourinho had been captured by TV cameras grimly heading for the changing rooms, a few minutes before the half-time interval. The ITV commentator suggested that the result would depend on what the gifted coach could do to change the performance of the ailing team.

From the start of second half, Chelsea upped their game. Within a few minutes their increased pressure was followed by a goal. If there is such a thing as momentum within a sporting contest, Chelsea had achieved it and was benefiting from it. A goal for either side would win the two-leg tie, and the team would advance into the quarter-finals of the European Cup. A well-worked goal from Captain Michael Ballack was the inevitable winner.

Victory had been billed as a critical factor for the team to achieve its lofty aspirations, following the three years of bank-rolling by billionaire owner Roman Abramovitch. Speculation had been growing that Mourinho's future at the club was in doubt regardless of the result, although failure would have reduced his chances even more.

Mourinho was happy to explain subsequently what happened at half-time. His team appeared to need a jolt to help them out of a psychologically bad place.

"I asked the players to enjoy the situation," Mourinho said of his half-time team talk. "We had 45 minutes to change things, and I asked them 'are you scared of it or are you going to enjoy it?'... Psychologically, I just made the players think a little bit."

How might we explain the change in the team's performance? One explanation fits with the charismatic model of leadership. The great leader inspires his followers through his own personality and stirring performance. The overall impact extends far beyond the words, to the instantaneous impression created by the leader.

According to that sort of thinking, the result of the leader's 'speech act' was to trigger an immediate change in behaviour in the players. Through his shrewd psychological insight, and 'giving them something to think about' the players responded.

If we look a little more carefully, we may feel there are other factors to consider. Both Mourinho and the opposing coach Jesualdo Ferreira felt that another change had also been important. At half-time, Jon Obi Michel was introduced, giving Chelsea the dynamism lacking from mid-field. The credit for the change still goes to the coach, but the impact of his words have to be considered alongside the impact of his insightful decision.

The situation is complex and unclear, suggesting that it is some combination of the substitution of Michel, and the half-time leadership intervention which taken together achieved the desired change. Some leaders may have hit on a tactical shift to help put things right at half-time. Other leaders might have well-developed psychological sensitivity (emotional intelligence?). I suggest that the combination of tactical astuteness and psychological astuteness is particularly rare.

So, yes, I'd say that the overall impact Mourinho had on the result was in this instance significant, and also one likely to have been matched by only minority of coaches at any level of the game.

There is an important point here for wannabe leaders in football and beyond.

Mourinho acknowledges how much he learned strategically and tactically from his mentor, the former England coach Bobby Robson with whom he started his career at Porto. The half-time team-talk has a ring to it that sounds equally authentic if we imagine it had been delivered by Sir Bobby.

This is evidence which suggests that leadership performance on the Football field can be learned and developed, even by a special one such as José Mourinho.

But what of the rest of us? Among the less gifted, those who believe they can learn such things from their role models are probably right. Those who believe they can't … well they are also probably right as well.

Trust me

April 21 2007

Renewed rumours had broken out at the start of the 2007-8 that relations between owner and coach at Chelsea had deteriorated. The climate there was at best a London luke-warm and at worse a Russian Steppes shivering cold.

Speculation has been rife for nearly a year that José Mourinho will lose his job as Chelsea coach at the end of the season.

Chelsea's influential CEO Peter Kenyon announces that Mourinho's job is safe. This does nothing to halt the rumours.

When a politician says "I'm not standing for leader" the message is rarely taken at face-value. I'm most familiar with the UK scene, but it seems a pretty universal reaction.

We can examine this through the incident in which Peter Kenyon tried to dismiss rumours that José Mourinho will be fired at the end of the year.

Even interviews by team captain John Terry denying any truth to the story did not prevent the rumours from continuing.

Kenyon could hardly have been more specific. In an interview published on the club's website he was reported as saying: 'José's got a contract until 2010 and we're not going to sack him. He's got the full support of the board, that's really important'.

My suspicion is, that Mourinho's departure is more than media gossip. One broader issue is the attraction to many journalists to keep a good story running. Some have made claims to know 'exclusively' that José Mourinho is going, with 'exclusive' news of yet another celebrity coaching star who has already been approached to replace him.

Germany's National coach Jürgen Klinsmann is the latest of a long line of heirs apparent to be mentioned. There's little mileage in writing a headline saying 'Manager to stay'.

In Football, the view of the club's owner is often paramount. In the case of Chelsea, owner Roman Abramovich has about as much power as any one person can wield. Whatever Kenyon says, and even if José's got a contract to 2010, and even if he has the full support of the board today ... well, you can fill in the dots for yourself. If Mr Abramovich is finding José irritating to deal with, he will have no problem with disposing of his turbulent manager'

Mourinho's record at Chelsea over the last three years has been outstanding. Before his arrival he had already established himself as one of the most successful coaches in world football. This gives credibility to his somewhat ironic self-description as The Special One. He has recently made it clear that he would like to stay at the club, implying that tany decision to leave would not be of his making.

Leadership is often said to be the process of influencing others in seeking to achieve one's goals. Kenyon would like to influence fans, as well as the media, into believing that Mourinho will stay. 'There is no 'José Mourinho problem' at Chelsea he insists. At times, even making such a statement signals that the speaker may be acting more out of defending a position, than out of a wish to provide accurate information

José Mourinho seems to be achieving that precious asset of trust in his relationship with his players. He has communicated his belief that the players, too, are 'special ones'. When needed, a half-time gee-up from the Coach (coupled with shrewd and sometimes daring substitutions) has been followed in the second half by a return to the high levels of performance demanded of the players.

Charismatic leaders achieve their results partly through a form of unconditional trust that they induce in followers. 'Less special ones' have to rely on force of argument, often against the reluctance of others to believe what they are being told.

We should take a look at the pattern of behaviours of the actors. In the past, Kenyon has tended to be regarded as brilliant and visionary business executive and one with 'safe pair of hands'.

On the other hand, the role of a Corporate spokesperson is to present the view the company wants presenting. My assumption (and I guess this shared by the journalists developing the 'José is on his way out' story) is that Mourinho has been pushing his employers to get his own way. He believes he is the best and that no-one would want to get rid of him. Which may not be the view of an owner who is not prepared to be bullied.

Postscript

Why were Peter Kenyon's assertions not taken as a definitive end to speculation about José 's retention as Chelsea's manager?

I see now that I was too pre-occupied with the alleged rift between José Mourinho and Chelsea's owner Roman Abramovich. The tone of my writing suggests that the main consideration in José staying or leaving was his (allegedly) worsening relationship with Roman Abramovich.

If I had followed my own advice given to business students, I would have looked more carefully at other factors that might explain what was happening and maybe glimpse possibilities into the future. In this specific instance, I needed to take more into account background information readily available at the time.

Manchester United supporters will have been aware that Peter Kenyon had joined Chelsea in 2003 as part of Roman Abramovich's upgrade of the club's players and staff.

He had been acquired after a successful and loyal career at the club where he had been appointed chief executive in August 2000. His move to Chelsea was seen as controversial as he had previously proclaimed himself as a lifelong Manchester United supporter.

During his first years at Chelsea his business acumen continued to be evident. He was reported as being involved in the unsuccessful attempt to recruit Sven-Göran Eriksson from his post as England manager before Mourinho's appointment. Kenyon was personally committed to hiring Mourinho.

If he had infuriated MUFC fans with his own move to Chelsea, he later a similar effect on Arsenal fans in the poaching of Ashley Cole, their international defender. In 2005 a £300,000 fine had been imposed on Chelsea by the Premier League for breaking league regulations. Fines were also imposed on José Mourinho and Ashley Cole although these were reduced on appeal

The press would have been aware of the black arts of the political denial when a statement is made such as 'the club has complete faith in its manager'. They would have also seen the swift change of alliance by Kenyon from MUFC to Chelsea, and the various poaching initiatives. Their suspicions would have been based on more than an owner's irritation with a disputatious manager.

At the time of writing I might have commented on evidence of the cut-throat nature of the football business, and Peter Kenyon's willingness to transfer his loyalties with the pragmatism that is sometimes described as Machiavellian.

Later, in October 2009, and shortly after Mourinho's first departure as Manager, Peter Kenyon also quit his chief executive role

Football correspondent Jason Burt of *The Telegraph* suggested that there had been a wider power struggle going on at Chelsea since José 's time. The players in the struggle appear as pawns moved around by the owner.

One key figure was the brilliant Danish footballer and sporting director Frank Arensen who had been brought into Chelsea by Abramovich in a contentious fashion from Tottenham Hotspur. According to Burt, Peter Kenyon was strongly in favour of retaining Mourinho while Frank Arensen took a different view. Now Arensen seemed to have taken a step forwards:

'Arnesen will act as the board's liaison with manager Carlo Ancelotti and deal with the football side of the business ... The changes mean Abramovich is dispensing with a high-profile, highly-paid chief executive and running the club himself.

It also appears that Kenyon has become the victim of a classic Russian business practice – marginalise an employee so that he is given less and less responsibility and, inevitably, decides that the situation is untenable and walks out.'

The description of a power struggle seems convincing to me, but I would be more inclined to see the story as one to have been played out not just as a 'classic Russian business practice', but in many organizations ancient and modern.

Destiny

September 20 2007

José Mourinho leaves Chelsea football club at sets of for Italy as coach of Inter Milan. In doing so, he fulfils his destiny as the special one, chosen to achieve greatness. In a moment of gloom, I wrote that his story, like that of David Beckham, is the tragedy of those who would challenge the Gods by flying too close to the sun.

José Mourinho is the John F Kennedy of football mangers. The similarities to the careers of David Beckham and George Best at Manchester United are worth noting.

According to the mythologists, any powerful story draws on deep and widely shared beliefs about ourselves and our world.

It speaks of our acceptance of powerful forces guiding our destiny. The most powerful stories are told and retold down the ages. They can be found in Greek tragedies, in Celtic and Norse sagas, and also in the campfire tales of ancient peoples. The central figure is heroic, destined to succeed spectacularly, and then fail just as dramatically. The message is that the special ones may appear to have been blessed, but whatever supernatural force is out there doing the blessing also wants to remind us humans that at some point we have to come to terms with our limitations.

The special gifts of the charismatic individual include the ability to be captivating those with whom they come into contact. We still use the old terms such as 'spell-binding' about their acts and speeches.

José had to go. He was fated to lead Chelsea to success, as he was fated to win the European Cup with Porto, a team hardly considered capable of it. Charismatic leaders have that effect on followers. The spell makes players believe they too are capable of achieving things they would otherwise have believed to be impossible.

Those who come to mock, often fall under the spell, hard as they may struggle against it.

Mourinho has even captivated the skilled and wilful members of the English Media legions, although there were always those waiting, waiting patiently for the story to end in José's downfall.

'José has a contract to 2010. He will be staying at Chelsea'. Thus spake Peter Kenyon on behalf of the club. But the fact that he needed to make such an assurance was significant.

Perhaps sensitized by the week's financial denials and reversals of policy by the Government and the Bank of England, I was not convinced by the spokesman on behalf of the Chelsea financial empire.

So much so that I found time yesterday to update the previous post.

As is it with José, so it was with David Beckham and George Best I mused. Their stories have similar ingredients of great giftedness and achievements accompanied by reminders of their fallibility, and potential downfalls. All achieved world-wide acclaim. All suffered.

George Best tragically is no longer with us. José and David still may have opportunities to play out further episodes in their next stages of their personal Odysseys.

In hindsight: I left unsaid why I thought the three footballing figures were following a shared path from triumph to disaster so familiar in mythology and in the accepted trajectory of charismatic leaders.

The post was a written as a personal reaction to the departure of José from Chelsea. I had obviously accepted his frequent public declarations of his deep and lasting love for the club and its supporters.

David Beckham does not fit a charismatic leadership profile as neatly as does Mourinho. He is arguably closer to that of an iconic figure, a global super-celebrity. The distinction I am making is that Beckham has buckets load of charisma, as evidenced by his multiple glamorous achievements. But Mourinho shares with charismatic leaders the power to influence through his words. One of many examples would be the half-time talk described earlier which seems to have galvanized his team to victory.

George Best has been described as the first iconic cultural icon from the world of football. His lifestyle contributed to his tragic early death. While Beckham has enjoyed as glamorous a lifestyle as Best, I am not sure now why I described him in such tragic terms in the original post. On reflection, it might have been better to suggest that Beckham has coped remarkably well with the downside of being a global celebrity.

One cultural commentator noted that 'Beckham had become part of a tabloid cartoon couple, Posh and Becks, amassed a family fortune, caused mass hysteria in Asia, Africa and wherever his playing career took him; given rise to various dubious hairstyles; launched fragrances; become a sex symbol for straight women and a pin-up for gay men'.

Not the best example, then of a man tragically ruined by his fame. I suppose I was stumbling towards the idea that however rich and powerful you are, you may still find there are disappointments in life and unfulfilled ambitions. For Mourinho, there is the restlessness and sometimes necessity to move clubs leaving behind unresolved conflicts. For Abramovich, it is the still unfulfilled quest to build a football club that will be remembered as among the greatest of football dynasties. For Beckham it was as much success on the football field as off it. He might have achieved this at Manchester United.

His manager, Alex Ferguson, himself a charismatic figure, concluded that Brand Beckham was in danger of being seen as bigger than the club, and David had to go. His subsequent wanderings were signs of his own unfulfilled ambitions as his career wound.

A similar concern seemed to have been around at Barcelona in 2008 when the club decided to appoint Pep Guardiola as manager, although José had also put himself forward for the position.

Mourinho Tipped as next England Manager

December 14 2007

This brief post was published after José had moved from Chelsea to Inter Milan. He was considered, but eventually not appointed, as manager of the England football team.

Following Steve McLaren's departure, Mourinho emerged as the strong favourite to become his successor as England manager, in the media and among many football supporters.

BBC Radio 5 Live football correspondent Mike Ingham noted:

"In many ways he would have been perfect if the job is about giving players an extra 10% and I think he would have done that. Mourinho ticked all the boxes bar one – I'm not sure how much of a diplomat he would have been".

He might had added on behalf of a minority of fans, "… pity he's not English".

The Guardian considered that Mourinho was the FA's first choice, though Soho Square sources [FA headquarters] say that he was never offered the job. The impression is that the FA establishment remain uncertain of José's reliability.

The FA's caution was borne out when talks between Mourinho's agent, Jorge Mendes, and the FA director of football, Sir Trevor Brooking, ended with José ruling himself out.

Three weeks later, and another of the world's super coaches, Fabio Capello, was appointed to the post. The prospects of José becoming England's manager had faded away.

Inter Regnum

May 22 2010

José 's rule as manager of Inter Milan was a triumph in terms of results. His victory of Bayern Munich delivered the European Champions cup to Inter. It was the trophy he had been brought to Chelsea for and which he had failed to win.

The mighty Bernabau Stadium, home of Real Madrid, erupted as the champions of Italy and Germany appeared on to the field. The Internationale side coached by José Mourinho were favourites to win. Bayern Munich, were recovering from a lull in their fortunes, under the coaching regime introduced by Louis van Gaal.

The final was yet another critical point in the careers of the two managers. Van Gaal had been Mourinho's mentor at Barcelona. Their paths were to cross later as they both went on to future successes, but both struggled to survive, as we will see, with two different clubs in the English Premier league, five years later.

Mourinho had already had considerable gratification in the progress of Bayern in the competition. In the quarter finals they disposed of Chelsea who had disposed of José, arguably for his failure to win the self-same trophy. In the Semi-finals Bayern had won against Barcelona, another club considered by Mourinho to have spurned his merits in favour of Pep Guardiola earlier in his career

Van Gaal and Mourinho are both master strategists, committed to attacking only from soundly built defensive formations. Their managerial track records are comparable, as a BBC report pointed out:

'Mourinho has won six league titles in three countries, plus eight domestic trophies, a Uefa Cup and a Champions League. It is a CV that would cast those of most other managers into the shade, but not Van Gaal's.

The 58-year-old Dutchman has seven league titles in three countries to his name, plus seven domestic trophies, a Uefa Cup,

*two Super Cups, an Intercontinental Cup and a Champions
League triumph. He also managed the Netherlands for two
years, although the Dutch team failed to qualify for the 2002
World Cup during his tenure'.*

The final was to prove an evenly matched contest. Van
Gaal's descriptions of Mourinho's tactics as largely defensive
proved partly accurate, although as van Gaal would also have
anticipated, they were interspaced with counter-attacking forays.

Bayern's more aggressive style was neutralised, and
eventually it was Inter, the counter-attacking team, that scored,
rather against the run of play. As another BBC report put it:

*'With Robben giving left-back Christian Chivu a torrid time
and Mark van Bommel pulling the strings in midfield, the
Germans almost completely dominated...Then, on 34 minutes,
came Inter's ambush, Milito nodding Inter keeper Julio Cesar's
long clearance down to Schneider and then dashing on to the
Dutchman's smart return to clip home a delightful finish.'*

Mourinho's muted celebrations highlighted his awareness that
it was a lead which his side barely deserved.

The pattern continued in the second half. Bayern's wing
attacks repeated threatened. Mourinho was increasingly agitated
on the sidelines, as the Bayern supporters roared encouragement
for their team.

Then another lightening quick movement from the
Argentinian Diego Milito, this time scoring himself. There was
no time for Bayern to respond. Mourinho's team had won. The
two managers exchanged surprisingly warm embraces.

But even in victory, Mourinho's subsequent farewells to the
Inter supporters from the pitch were interpreted as evidence that
the rumours were true. They knew for sure that he would be
leaving Inter soon to return to the Bernabau as manager of the
mighty Real Madrid

Why did José leave Inter?

May23 2010

Why did José quit Inter Milan immediately after the season of his greatest success there? My personal archives showed a gap about much of his time in Milan. A famous headline many years ago demonstrated an attitude in England which still prevails: 'Heavy fog in channel continent cut off'

Much the same attitude exists today towards football matches in which no English team is involved, (although this has changed rapidly as the transfer market opened up so substantially in the last few years and European-wide sharing of the top league matches became a possibility each weekend).

To find out more of what had happened in my period of personal isolation from José, I needed to go back to the news accounts of the period 2008-2010.

Italy's domestic league had some notoriety through scandals involving various form of creative rule-breakings. The most notable of these, *the calciopoli* (football corruption) scandal broke at a time of highest international exposure as Italy was preparing to play Germany in Berlin in 2006 in the World Cup final. Italian clubs in the premier division, including AC Milan (owned by Silvio Berlusconi), Lazio and Juventus, had been found guilty of extensive match rigging and received a range of punishments including relegation to Serie B, exclusion from European competitions, and the stripping of recently won titles.

Inter Milan, the club José was to join, did not suffer these indignities. Indeed, they had just won the league as a result of the weakened opposition through bans and sand demotions.

Roberto Mancini who left Inter as Mourinho arrived in 2008, had won three successive Serie A championships. That had not been enough for him to retain his job. Inter wanted more than any other footballing goal to with the European Champions Cup. Roman Abramovich at Chelsea had been waiting seven years for the trophy that even José had not been able to deliver. Inter had been yearning after the greatest prize in European football for forty- five years.

Des Kelly writing for the Daily Mail Online gives an explanation of José's impact on Italian football as Inter arrives at Stamford Bridge for a vital European Cup match in February, to face a Chelsea team now managed by Carlo Ancelotti

'*Mourinho is regarded as just too corrosive a character in a league just beginning to recover from the Calciopoli scandal of 2006. Mourinho has no hesitation in exploiting this whenever results or referees' decisions go against Inter, blaming wholesale corruption in officialdom for any setbacks. Mourinho has been hit with a three-match touchline ban and £40,000 fine, which is being viewed as the beginning of a long and acrimonious departure from Serie A for the Portuguese coach. A top Italian writer, who deals with the Inter camp daily, said: 'We don't think he will be here next season and we won't be sorry about that. There are plenty of people around who will drive him to the airport.'*

Mourinho had indicated interest in a return to the Premier League. Kelly guessed (rightly) that José was already planning to leave Inter for Real Madrid.

Fixture Shift

April 1 2008

The great financial crisis of 2008 was approaching. In the spirit of All Fools' Day, on April 1st, I found myself writing about a dream in which Alan Greenspan then head of America's Federal Reserve Bank appears as host and caller on a radio chat show about football.

The background to the post is displeasure expressed by Chelsea with the Football Association as a consequence of rearranged fixtures believed to put at risk the club's title bid. Any resemblance of other characters in the dream to living or dead individuals, is coincidental.

Falling asleep with a well-known sports and new programme filtering into my slumbers, I had a curious dream for All Fools Day. It was something to do with a football phone-in programme. It involved a radio broadcaster Alan Greenspan. His first call in my dream came from a Chelsea supporter who only identified himself as Dave.

Dave: Hi Alan, how are you?

Alan Greenspan: I'm fine Dave …

Dave: …Good, good, Alan. I'm fine too.

Alan: What's your point, Dave?

Dave: I'm calling about the atrocious and unfair decision by the Muppets at the FA. They've done it again. It's madness.

Alan: Dave, before you go any further… can you turn your radio down? It's distorting the signals from the marketplace … That's better, thanks, I can hear you now. Where are you calling from?

Dave: Sorry. Right. Yeah, I'm back home from the match.

Alan [testily]: What's your point Dave? We've got thousands of fans trying to place their calls.

Dave: What's my point? Another stupid seven thirty kick-off time. That's my point. What sort of time is that Alan? Who decides these things? What's going on?

Alan: You mean the decision to switch the central bank's policy to prop up the financial markets?

Dave: No Alan. I mean the switch of the date of Chelsea Everton game. I can make my point in two words. *Big business.* No-one cares about the real fans any more... Football always used to be played three o'clock Saturday. Every week of the season. Home games, a couple of drinks with the lads, then down The Bridge for kick-off. My dad used to take me. Now it's any time except 3 o'clock. It's late morning, or eight o'clock in the evening, Alan. It's every day of the week.

Alan: Dave, Dave. No one's been saying that louder than me. Call me a life-long libertarian republican if you like, but I've been consistent. I've been banging on since the start of The Premier league... So what's your point?

Dave: My point is this. As I said to your researcher. This disgraceful, crass, stupid, malicious decision over Everton. That's my point. Even the morons at the FA have put our entire season in jeopardy. What's going on? You tell me? would they have done it to Man U.? I think not. Ferguson wouldn't let it happen to them, would he?

Alan: Listen, Dave. I'm the first to say it when I see attempts to influence market forces. But I don't agree with you on this one. It's not Fergie influencing the FA. (And it's the Premier League actually).

Listen. Let me say this. You got it spot on, when you said it was all about Big Business. Everything is about Big Business. But You have to think credit conditions. They aren't good at the moment, Dave. And credit is the real engine of capitalism.

Dave: My point entirely, Alan. And why do they leave it so late to tell us? Now we get to play Wigan. No big deal I grant you. But that's on the Monday night and then we got to travel up to Liverpool on play Everton on the Thursday for an eight o'clock kick-off. It's crazy. It's lunacy. They've gone bleeding barking out of control.

Alan: Not to mention the ridiculous Easter Sunday timing of your game with Arsenal. So that turned out fine, when you won. But we can't say *a postiori* it was a rational decision to screen it without considering the possibility that government interference restricted the freedom of capital market operations in the city.

But we must move on. Thanks for your call Dave. We've got Sadiq on the line. He's waiting patiently in a traffic jam on the M1.

Hello Sadiq. What's your point …?'

Then I woke up and checked the fixture problem. As a statement on the Chelsea Website put it:

'Chelsea is extremely disappointed with the announcement regarding the Everton fixture. We believe the decision to hold the match on Thursday April 17 undermines the sporting integrity of the competition by giving our rivals for the Premier League title an unnecessary competitive advantage at a critical time of the season, with more recovery time from their previous match and preparation time for their next fixture when we have to play two games during the same period.

Secondly there has been no consideration given to our fans who will be presented with serious travel, work and other issues. And lastly, the decision sets a dangerous precedent in changing match days still further when fixture congestion does not exist and when a sensible solution regarding other television matches that weekend was suggested.

Football has benefited greatly from the backing of television and Chelsea as much as anyone else. However, this decision is one step too far and we reserve all rights on our position'.

The announcement threw no light on to the interesting question of who decides what when such a decision is made. Police concerns, fixture complexities, fans' travelling arrangements all come into consideration, as does juggling of rights claimed by the competing television broadcasters on the football authorities of the FA and the Premier League. This year, the Premiership rights have been split between Sky Sports and Setanta.

A little digging reveals that the fixture changes have already been announced on the Sky schedules. These disputes have emerged as football moved into an increasingly commercialised era. In earlier times all weekend league football matches in England were played at 3pm on Saturday. This arrangement at first made sense to accommodate the shift patterns of workers who would flock to the support of their local team after the Saturday morning shift.

Later, as matches were broadcast on radio, and then televised, the 3pm kick-off for all Saturday matches was protected, and television prohibited.

This was a typical English compromise, justified through the assumption that attendance at minor league matches would decline as supporters would prefer to stay at home to watch blurry black and white flickering images on television.

In 1960, the first live football league match was broadcast by ITV between Blackpool and Bolton Wanderers. The match was played at 6-50 pm (17.50) but not broadcast until 7.30pm (19.30). This was again a decision to prevent fans staying away from the 3pm kick off matches, as it enabled fans to get home in time for the televised treat.

The debate about 'Commercial broadcasting of football league persisted, and it was not until 1983 that another league match was broadcast, again by ITV (Tottenham Hotspur v Nottingham Forest).

The conservatism of the football authorities in England was overcome by the seismic shift caused by the formation of the Premier League which secured the first of the lucrative rights deals, with the Sky Sports arm of Rupert Murdoch's media empire.

The earlier restriction to broadcasting of the Saturday afternoon football fixtures was preserved. There were gestures towards the protection of fans of the minor league clubs from the attraction of televised broadcasts of the glamour clubs of the Premier League. But this was to prove little more than a fig leaf preserving the football establishment from total embarrassment.

The number of matches played untelevised at 3pm on Saturday declined, and the 'weekend' schedules spread to other times on Saturday, and then include Sunday matches, and eventually into the following week.

The commercial broadcasters offered ever-increasingly attractive deals to televise the top games live. The arms race had begun towards monster wages for the best international players.

This approaching capitulation to the commercialization of football was defended by a Premier League spokesperson:

'The compilation of the fixture list is a complex procedure.

It faces enormous pressure from international match and European competition dates, as well as the need to balance the important requirements of the police and our broadcasters.

We are also required by the European Commission to televise 138 matches per season, which brings its own inevitable pressures.'

This may have some relevance, but only indirectly addresses Dave's more specific point in my dream about the changes to the timing of Chelsea's fixtures, and the general lack of concern about the problems of the fans.

It seems to me Dave is suffering as a result of a power struggle between competing interests of the media, and the Premier The European Champions cup, was also growing in marketability so that EUFA also became involved.   As organizers of the biggest competition of all, The World Cup, EUFA's parent organisation FIFA exercised indirect influence on scheduling of matches at a national level.

When you think about it, the sorting out of football fixtures for people like Dave makes the sub-prime crisis easy enough for someone like Alan Greenspan to deal with.

Postscript:

Scheduling of matches is complex, but arguably a irritant for fans and football clubs. The original post published in *Leaders We Deserve* under-estimated the impact months away of the global financial crash starting in 2008.

Differentials between the haves and have nots in football continued. Clubs like Chelsea benefitted disproportionately. Smaller fry were to go into receivership in increasing numbers.

Inverting the Pyramid

June 2 2008

Inverting the Pyramid: A History of Football Tactics. written by football journalist Jonathan Wilson has become established as a football classic, winning the Football Book of the Year award in 2009. The book was published during the time when José Mourinho was adding his own footnote to the subjects of tactics and formations at Chelsea. The review was revised and updated in 2015.

Inverting the Pyramid has the scholarship of an academic reference text, complete with rigorous indexing and reference sources. It traces how the early leisure-time occupation of football in the public schools of England became systematized and spread around the world to its present form. Rules were needed to permit fair contests; fairness being particularly valued throughout the far-flung British Empire.

The amateur contests of the nineteenth century produced rudimentary tactics to gain one side an advantage. Inter-passing between players emerged, as did skills of running forward while controlling the ball, later known as dribbling. Above all, the romantic idea of all players attacking was replaced with allocating a few players to defend against attacks.

The emerging rules had established eleven as the number of players in a team. From this, the original great pyramid of football became stablished, with five players as an attacking line closest to enemy forces, (the forwards) three players behind them (midfielders), and the two defenders or full backs ahead of the goalkeeper.

A goal is scored if the ball when in play passes the goal line legally. (Yes, many readers know all that. I cling to the belief that there may be readers who have no experience or understanding of the information conveyed in this paragraph. These would include aliens preparing to relocate among us, escapees from sects where access to the outside world is prohibited, and assorted often blissfully happy individuals whose obsessions exclude attention paid to the beautiful game.)

Anyway, as Wilson points out, the structure or arrangement of the players in a game emerged. At first there was no need for distinguishing it from other structures. You just played not knowing about labels or other places to position yourself.

You didn't know that the players lined up in what could be seen as a kind of flat pyramid. The goal and goal keeper were at the pointy end of the pyramid. Then there were two defensive players close enough to chat with the goalkeeper, three ahead of them in the middle of the formation (who known not surprisingly as midfielders) and five attackers ahead who started a game close to the half-way line as possible with the intention of advancing through the ranks of the opposing team.

So you really had two great pyramids arranged like troops to do battle. The newer systems were mostly ways of strengthening the defence at the expense of the attack. Various versions were tried. A labelling system came into use to explain the variants, based on the numbers of players in the different lines.

The original arrangement was given a name to distinguish it from fancy new-fangled arrangements. Because football theorists even in those days were to be found to the geeky side of the classroom, labels took on a classification system resembling the wheel sizes of steam engines.

[Note: As a boy I was one such geek equipped with notebook to write down the 4-4-2 formation of Atlantic Class locomotives, the closest to the classical 2-3-5 arrangement of the great football pyramid. For the really pedantic, I should add that the classification of engine wheels as established by Mr W.H. White start with the front wheels not the back. The Atlantic Class engines as a football system would have been a 2-4-4 system.]

The 2-3-5 system in football if not in steam engine classifications was still around at the highest levels of the game, long after the tactical innovation developed by Herbert Chapman of Arsenal in the 1930s had produced kinks in the classical lines, looking like a 'W' in defence behind an 'M' in attack. Confused? Yes, you have to squint a bit but the line-up then looks like a M in defence and a W in attack, but that's the goalkeeper's view.

Incidentally, the goal keeper gets ignored by the football structure theorists, which possibly contributes to a reputation for weirdness in goalkeepers, and a deep desire among some of their number to go forward and score a winning goal in the dying moments of a vital game.

The English football establishment had codified the game in the 1890s and just assumed he permanence of the 2-3-5 arrangement, later allocating numbers for positions on the field of play as well as on shirts.

The numbering of players by location on the field remained, even when the pyramid started its transformation and the defensive line accumulated more players and the attackers diminished in numbers.

Chapman's W M system was a 3-4-3 formation. Purists in England brought up on flying wingers did not appreciate the disappearance of the flank excursions and the set-up was seen as a move away from an era of attacking play.

The game that shook the traditionalists of out of nostalgia and complacency was a crushing loss by England to a Hungarian international team in the 1950s. The Magyars had brilliant individual players, one of whom, Puskas, was to become a legend in the world of football.

More importantly, England, the spiritual home of Football, had to take seriously more radical possibilities emerging than the tinkering with the traditional pyramid that the W M system offered.

The Hungarians played as if they came from a different planet, indicating the potential for creating new ways of attacking through complex structures. But the pyramid had been loosened rather than inverted. This was also the case with the ideas re-imported from Brazil and the other Latin American teams who were deploying structures which encouraged individual flair.

The fluidity appealed, but the wider European change had already come with the development of the controversial 'lock down' system in Italy known as Catenaccio, the chain or as the English traditionalists thought of it, the ball and chain, shackling attempts to break a defence.

Catenaccio according to Wilson had four defenders, a line of three midfielders, and three forwards, 'similar to the modern 4-3-3 as practiced by, say, Chelsea in José Mourinho's first two seasons at the club'. The approach was clearly giving the old pyramid a tilt toward its inverted form.

Another reference source mentioned José's system at Chelsea (in his first and highly successful time there) as a more defensively executed 4-5-1.

An interesting aspect of Catenaccio was its justification at first as 'the right of the weak' to frustrate stronger opposition. The first major team to embrace it effectively was Internationale in Milan, the team which Mourinho coached to success many years later, with perhaps the style identified by author Wilson as José's system at Chelsea.

As football became more global, attacking systems encouraging individual flair clashed with defensive ones like the stifling Catenaccio.

According to Wilson, the invincibility of the Catenaccio system was eventually overcome by crushing defeats from attacking systems such as the fondly-remembered win by the Scottish team Celtic against Internationale in the European League cup final of 1966, and subsequently by victories in the hands (or should I say feet) of the great Liverpool teams of the era.

The final chapters of the book take the reader to the late 20th century and beyond. The classic pyramid of attack is now well and truly dismantled. The simple basic premise of the book is justified.

Wilson is wise enough to recognize the diversity of structures in today's total football. Perhaps he could have examined more the phenomenon of globalization and the various innovations connected with technological and medical advances.

He can hardly be criticized for failing to anticipate the corruption scandals that would bring about the disruption and possible destruction of the great power pyramids of FIFA and its European subsidiary UEFA.

Postscript:

I now see more clearly that the great Liverpool sides of the seventies and eighties and the Manchester United sides from the later Alex Ferguson era were routinely set out as a flexible and dynamic 'inverted pyramid'.

This involved a skilful and attacking midfielder 'playing in the hole' behind a traditional centre forward. Kevin Keegan operating just behind John Toshack for Liverpool would be a good example. One of my favourite pairings would be Eric Cantona playing behind Mark Hughes for Manchester United.

Bobby Robson when England manager famously deployed a similar system successfully in the 1986 World Cup with selecting Peter Beardsley supporting Gary Lineker.

My review also referred briefly to the importance of Total Football, to which Wilson devotes nearly a chapter. The structure of Total Football might be seen as a modern inverted pyramid. But the term is used to refer to a baffling and flexible attacking approach originating in the play of the all-conquering Hungarians in the 1950s and the brilliant Dutch teams master-minded by Johan Cruyff in the 1970s and 1980s.

More seriously, I had been so beguiled by Wilson's historical account of the public school traditions that I missed the significance of football as the working-class game recognised by managers including Bill Shankly at Liverpool, Matt Busby at Manchester United, and Bobby Robson for England and later on returning to Newcastle, all of whom grasped the point that, as one reviewer commented to me:

'life had few pleasures for the working man. Busby wanted his team to play entertaining football and give him (it was virtually all men in those days) something to look forward to and be excited about. Hence the Manchester United emphasis on fast action and attacking football which of course dictated the types of player recruited and team layout.'

A reviewer gave a vivid account of how a formation could be used as the 'prerogative of the weak' as the Italian originators of Catennacio understood the system to thwart the free-flowing-movement of their opponents.

'I remember conversations I had with a former captain of a Premiership team. He would reflect on his successful career and would discount the over-complication of team formations. He argued the merits of KISS (Keep It Simple, Stupid), saying that - expanding that complicated football formations cause more problems than offer solutions. I remember him suggesting 'new' formations were a little like fashion. Popularity comes and goes although the fundamentals of football remain the same.

He was laughing when he said how easy it is to confuse footballers. They need clear instructions to understand what is expected of them and what their role is in the team.

He tried to focus around the skills and competencies of the footballers such as Individual accountability, work ethic and effort; commitment; professionalism.

He talked about senior players in the team having an influence on the younger players following their example. He referenced 'good pros' as the ones who turned up for training early, stayed behind later, looked after their physical condition, stayed out of the media spotlight.

Going back to The Inverted Pyramid, formations are of course very important, and they have their contribution to make.

If I use [my nine-year-old son] as an example, he is like lots of children playing for a local team on our local park pitches.

I regularly see how the kids struggle to understand the benefits of a football formation. They just gravitate towards the ball like a swarm of insects. This causes problems and restricts the potential of the team.

As they learn more about the game, they start to appreciate how each individual makes a different contribution to the team performance and how specialisation and team organisation helps deliver better results. Team formation is essentially the framework and visual representation of how the team is organised.

The faster lads will likely be better placed on the wing, or perhaps as strikers. The bigger more robust ones will maybe find themselves in midfield or defence.

Overall, the coach needs to look at his squad, choose a formation - and importantly a style of play that plays to the strengths of his players and then go with it. Sam [Allardyce] at

Bolton is famed for his 'long ball' which is where you have two banks of four sitting deep. For long periods in the game, Bolton would sit defending just on the edge of the 18yards box. Four defenders, with four midfielders sat close together. So you had two banks of four.

This formation is hard for any team to break down. Even if we played Chelsea or Manchester United, the advantage that they might have had through their very fast and tricky wingers would be nullified by what we were doing.

Critics (including Mourinho, by the way) would claim that Bolton had 'parked the bus' [i.e. they had put lots of men behind the ball making it difficult for any player to dribble though] When Bolton won possession we hit a long ball up to Kevin Davies, whose job was to either hold the ball up and wait for support, or simply gain territorial advantage and win a corner or a header.

Big Sam kept things simple at Bolton. His teams were very well organised, and everyone knew their job, and what was expected of them.'

I Remember, I remember a Servant Leader

August 2 2009

Dimly, I remember a story. It is about the life of a much-loved English football manager Bobby Robson. I wrote about it on the moving occasion of his funeral. I did not mention the formative influence that Bobby had as mentor to José Mourinho which is now added to the account.

Bobby Robson loved football and served it well. He will also be remembered for an outstanding life lived with respect and warmth to everyone he met.

His death came as no great surprise to countless friends and admirers around the World. He had witnessed a charity football match at the home of his beloved Newcastle United, one week ago [July 26th 2009].

A crowd of 33,000 turned out to honour former England and Newcastle manager Sir Bobby Robson at St James' Park. England XI including several members of Robson's 1990 World Cup squad took on a team of their German counterparts in a game to raise money for the 76-year-old's own cancer charity.

Robson, in a wheelchair as he battled cancer for a fifth time, was introduced to both teams and presented with a lifetime achievement award by before kick-off. The match, which began after a stirring rendition of Italia 90 anthem Nessun Dorma was intended as a replay of the World Cup semi-final in Turin famously won on penalties by West Germany. The match had been the highlights of Bobby Robson's career and an 'if only ...' moment ever since for England's football fans.

A week later he finally succumbed to his fifteen years of illness.

The numerous tributes on his death covered his sporting achievements which themselves would have warranted some international recognition. This outpouring of emotion was something else. The extra ingredient was for a life lived under intense media scrutiny.

Graham Taylor, his successor as England's Football Manager was deeply wounded by media intrusiveness and cruelty.

Typically, Bobby Robson rode out press attention and associated criticism apparently unmoved. It must be said that Robson less-savagely treated than was Graham Taylor, and most other subsequent managers of England.

Why might that have been the case? One of the less-explored ideas in business textbooks is that of the Servant Leader. The term is associated with work of Robert Greanleaf. The concept seems to be as admirable in theory as it is hard to live out in practice.

From time to time I have wondered about some of those nominated as examples of servant leaders such as Al Gore and Bill Gates. I remained rather unconvinced although Gates may have undergone some moral conversion perhaps through his wife's charitable interests.

The younger Bill Gates seemed to be somewhat unconcerned with deep ethical considerations as he pursued to goal of building Microsoft into a global empire. Al Gore, a politician of undoubted green credentials had not left me with strong primary evidence of something special in his earlier career.

The virtuous life is more likely to be espoused in some contexts than others. At one extreme, we might expect the values of servant leadership to match rather well in religious and educational contexts. Not so well in fiercely sporting contexts. And hardly at all well in business. Politics is a rather interesting case, with politicians careful to present themselves as utterly committed to service to the people, while too often demonstrating practices of blatant self-serving careerism.

There is something special about Bobby Robson's deeply held values. It seems to me it to come from a coherent set of behaviours which reflected deeply held values. His life story fits well with religious and ethical principles. But Bobby rarely invoked morality, or claimed a higher purpose for his actions. Rather, he displayed in them an enthusiasm for a life in football, but also with respect for the needs of people with whom he came into contact, particularly with the needs of young footballers on his teams.

[Another note for leadership students: There is much talk recently about a leader's moral compass and of authentic leadership. How well do you consider Bobby's story might help you explore these concepts?]

Robson's fight against cancer has become well-known. His charity follows the example set by another great football figure, Bobby Moore, who also died of the disease. The charities fund much-needed research. I happen to support them, and wish them well. But the academic in me resists the conclusion that founding a charity adds to our understanding of Bobby Robson.

I can do no better that quote the man himself, from an admirable BBC Obituary

'In his 2005 autobiography Farewell but not Goodbye, Robson said of the experience of receiving a civic honour "A number of [Newcastle City] councillors wrote to me to say they had never seen so much emotion in a ceremony of that kind. Perhaps it was because I had talked about my father, and how he went down the pit white and came up black, in an area where the two colours symbolise a city's love of football, a love that burns within me and will never fade." It is a fitting way to sum up Robson's obsession with the beautiful game.'

Postscript:

For once, an article about Bobby had omitted to mention his influence as mentor on the early career of José Mourinho. At the time, Robson had gained honours and respect for a career of a working class hero. He had won twenty international caps for England, and after a slow start to his managerial career demonstrated his tactical and man management skills notably in England with Ipswich Town, and later with a disputatious but talented bunch of players with the Dutch club PSV.

He joined the Portuguese club Sporting Lisbon and quickly saw the talents of the very bright, very engaging translator Mourinho. His reward for restoring the fortunes of the club was his abrupt dismissal by its capricious President.

Sporting's rivals, F.C. Porto, saw an opportunity, hired Robson, and accepted Mourinho as part of the deal. Porto promptly went on to beat Sporting in the Portuguese Cup to win League titles in successive seasons (1994-1996).

The successful pairing of Robson and Mourinho moved to Barcelona where further success was gained. Robson was voted European Manager of the Year for 1996–97as the club won three trophies including the European Cup Winners cup. Bobby's health was declining, and José's career was on its upward trajectory.

José never became manager at Barcelona. His initial admiration was to turn into bitterness during his period as manager of Barcelona's rivals Real Madrid

Mourinho Magic

December 3 2009

Charismatic leadership can be like a conjuring trick which seems to defy all rational principles. But there are limits to what can be achieved, as José Mourinho found out when he brought his Inter Milan team tot Old Trafford.

The European Cup tie was billed as the clash of two great football managers as José Mourinho brought his Inter Milan team to Old Trafford [Wed 11th March 2009] after a goalless first leg at Milan. Manchester United and Inter headed their respective national leagues. United had won the trophy in 2008, and had since won a fledgling competition to establish themselves as World Champions. Most commentators considered United to be the stronger of the two teams.

Inter had problems from injuries to key players. And yet there was a degree of caution in the press in predicting a winner. On the home goals rule, a score draw would be enough for Inter to go through. But the main consideration the pundits mentioned in favour of the Italian team was Mourinho's overwhelming winning record against Manchester teams (which means teams managed by Sir Alex Ferguson). This record, first with Porto, and then Chelsea, was part of the legend of Mourinho, the self-styled special one, and charismatic leader.

Mourinho may not have spooked Alex Ferguson, but he had had his usual effect at a distance, on supporters and media alike.

The first leg in Italy could be claimed as a minor victory for José. United played well but were denied by Inter in the first half, who then came back strongly after half time. Mourinho was assumed to have worked his magic during the interval on a team considered to have fewer world-class players in the prime of their careers.

The preservation of the image of a special one was captured in the post-match conference in Milan. Mourinho had, unusually, not acknowledged his counterpart on the touchline, when the match ended. This was not intended as a mark of disrespect.

'I have a special exit from the field', the special one explained. But he had left a message for Sir Alex with a 'three-hundred-pound bottle of wine' at his hotel, to say he would look forward to meeting at Old Trafford for the second leg.

Two weeks later, in the return leg at Manchester, Mourinho's customary swagger is evident as comes into view on the touchline wearing his trademark black cloak (sorry, overcoat).

The crowd in the theatre of dreams boo him energetically and theatrically. The contest starts.

Four minutes later, and José's magic spell seems to have gone wrong. Slack marking from Inter, and United take the lead. Technically Inter will still win if they score one goal and United do not add to their tally. Mourinho paces around uttering incantations.

But maybe he still has inspired something special in his players. Manchester's skill levels drop off. Afterwards, Ferguson was caustic about their sloppiness. His team gets to half-time lucky to preserve the lead.

United are still appearing scrappy and uncomfortable as the second half starts. Then United score another goal, in one of the few world-class moves of the game. Even then, with Inter now needing two goals to triumph, the players played nervously in a way that was at odds with the score, and their record at Old Trafford for many months.

United repelled fluent moves from their opponents, cameras switching from time to time to José on the touchline. As his team created chance after chance and failed convert them, his body language began to change. It was like watching one of those cartoon characters racing over a cliff, and pedalling furiously in mid-air before fantasy yields to the reality of gravity, and the character plunges to earth.

The crowd chanted 'You're not special anymore' but more with a mix of relief and black humour than of spite.

We were witnessing the limits of charisma. Maybe not gone for ever, but vanquished in one particular battle in one particular place. Even the magician's cloak looked more like a perfectly ordinary if expensive piece of clothing, more often associated with mourners at a funeral.

The final whistle blows. No special tunnel for José. The two managers execute a clumsy embrace for public consumption.

In the press conference shortly afterwards, José says Manchester United are 'at their maximum' and will win everything they compete for this year.

Of course they will. It takes super-special magic to defeat a chosen one.

John Terry and the Fake Shake

February 27 2010

A sad sporting leadership story shows how creativity can be a leader's secret weapon.

Every tale of leadership offers opportunities for learning. "How would I deal with that decision?" is a good question in the over-publicised case of John Terry and Wayne Bridge. There is also the question "What would I have done to avoid getting into mess in the first place?" For anyone not interested in football, you need to be aware that John Terry was recently stripped of the Captaincy of the England football team. The story had broken that he had been involved in an affair with the partner of former team-mate Wayne Bridge. Public interest is whipped-up again this week by the news that Bridges has decided not to take part in the up-coming World Cup.

Leaders We Deserve has regularly advocated the merits of creative leadership. How might this play out in practice? Take the critical incident being anticipated for today [February 27th, 2009].

Chelsea and Manchester City are due to play a football match. John Terry will be expected to lead out Chelsea (he retains the captaincy of that team). He will be expected to shake hands with members of the opposing team. So there we have a dilemma of leadership. What to do if the handshake is spurned? Oh, yes it's only a handshake. But for 'only a hand-shake' why is the story taking on huge significance, at least for journalists? That's another story, and one about symbolism and leadership.

How might creative leadership come into this? We can start with the assumption that dilemmas often result in either/or thinking. Break the 'either-or' and you have a chance of escaping the dilemma. I've also written about this as knight's move thinking. Edward de Bono would probably say it's where Lateral Thinking is needed.

The locked-in thinking presents the story as simply one man shaking hands with another. Suppose we pose it as 'how to arrange the pre-match handshakes between Chelsea and

Manchester City differently (in view of the unusual circumstances surrounding the event)'. I can think of several things that might happen. My thinking has switched from 'what Wayne Bridge must do' to 'what might Chelsea and Manchester City captains, players, and maybe supporters decide to do'. And, that is a matter of co-creativity, and distributed leadership. Whatever happens this afternoon at Stamford Bridge will be an opportunity for considering 'what might have been'.

Postscript:

At the start of the match, John Terry offered his hand to Wayne Bridge who rejects the proffered hand.

Chelsea fans boo Bridge enthusiastically throughout the game.

But another story was to supplant the hand-shake one. Chelsea lost at home 4-2. Two of their players were sent off by the referee. And I didn't notice a lot of creative leadership. The 'fake shake' gave the tabloids a few headlines the following day.

Dreams and Obsessions

April 28 2010

In advance of the semi-final of the European Champions Cup Tie between Inter Milan and Barcelona, José Mourinho offers his own philosophic take on the difference between the purity of his dreams, and Barcelona's obsessiveness.

The Special One continues on his special way. This time he suggests a difference between dreams and obsessions, and why his Internationale team will be less likely than their rivals Barcelona to be overwhelmed with psychological fantasies. In particular, he says that Barcelona are 'obsessed' with winning the Champions League at the Bernabeu, the home of their arch-rivals Real Madrid:

'I experienced what it is like [at Barcelona]. I have won cups -against Betis in 1997 - at the Bernabeu, where everyone was wrapped in Catalan flags. I know what it is about, it is anti-Madridismo. It is an obsession'.

At the time, I accepted what had been reported. That's the effect the charismatic leader has, even on someone like myself trying to understand its impact on listeners. There is a suspension of belief which lasts at least as long as the master is speaking.

Listeners are advised to figure out if there is any sense to what's being said, before getting too concerned ('obsessed'?) with what the great leader is up to.

Outside Mourinho world, dream contents are generally considered to be fantasy materials. Freud felt there was a scientific interpretation to much of what we are able to access in our dream-states. There are still many who offer and many who seek interpretations of dreams. The leadership literature has favoured the notion that a dream can articulate a desire and become a vision of the future. That seems a bit like José's point.

If he is suggesting that there are dreams ('pure') and obsessions ('impure') then I can't buy into the notion. Until new evidence is provided, (step forward the increasingly important neurologist as expert witness) I have to disagree. Dreams, particularly those connected with desires and visions, will have been generated though beliefs which may or may not have obsessional characteristics.

Probably if I had been listening as José was speaking I would have believed every word he said. His rival manager Pep Guardiola, was captain at Barcelona when Mourinho worked there under Bobby Robson. Pep is as cool as José is hot. So it's cool obsession against hot dreams.

A History of Charisma: Book Review

May 15 2010

A History of Charisma, by John Potts, Palgrave MacMillan, 2009 ISBN 9780 230 55153 4

If you like detective stories, you will enjoy *A History of Charisma* by Australian media scholar John Potts. I found myself reading it as a well-constructed and highly intelligent 'who done it'. It takes a skilful author to make such a page-turner based on a 'history of a word'. Potts has succeeded by writing in a lucid and intelligent style, sticking to a brief account of less than 300 pages, with a strong historical story line.

He fingers Saint Paul, one of the founders of the Christian church as the person who gave the word enormous significance. 'The term 'charisma' emerged in the early Christian church of the first century. It was eclipsed as a religious concept by the end of the third century...lay submerged for many centuries with intermittent appearances. [and] was reinvented in Max Weber's sociology in the early twentieth century' After an extensive study of popular and scholarly texts, Potts arrives at the view that the meaning of the word charisma has changed considerably from that of its original theological context. We learn that the roots of charisma can be traced to early Jewish and Graeco-Roman cultures and the ideas of gifts (we are familiar with the semantically-related term charity). Paul, educated in Greek' was aware of the concept of divine grace which had found its ways into Greek translations of Hebrew texts.

Paul gets a good idea. Or, as Potts writes, *'Paul Invents Charisma.'* Driven on by what Paul believed to be his divinely-ordained mission, he set about establishing his own vision for a religion that would survive and replace prevailing alternatives. He needed what in modern secular terms might be called a clear manifesto. He chooses to do this through a relabelling of older ideas under the new(ish) term which we now receive phonetically from the Greek as charisma.

Paul's manifesto was enormously successful at first, giving momentum to the growth and establishment of the institution of the early Christian church. Over time, however, there was a shift which saw "the rise of bishops, the demise of prophets … and transition from the rather free-wheeling Christian community of Paul's time to the structured ministry of the second-century." Charisma was to move to the margins of Church dogma, often becoming weakened by association with various contrarian views often castigated as heresies.

Which is where the term might have languished, if it had not been for the sociological writings of Max Weber. What might have remained a brilliant but obscure scholarly work in the original German in the 1920s, was translated into English and by the 1960s had become part of a popular (if misunderstood) discourse of bureaucracy and social change, including the role of leaders in traditional and modern societies.

Such was Weber's influence that it was assumed to carry with it the original conceptualisation of charisma, as an attribute of a special kind of revolutionary leader. For Potts, Weber misinterpreted the earlier Christian concept, replacing the notion of a spiritual gift bestowed on a community, to that of "a specific form of domination, an individual endowment used by remarkable leaders to command authority over their followers."

And so to modern times. A charismatic renewal has occurred since the 1960s as a religious movement. Evangelical Christians have rediscovered modes of worship finding strong appeal in The USA, but also internationally (South Korea's Yoido Full Gospel Church has been claimed to be the largest Christian community). Potts observed that the religious and secular outpourings with charismatic overtones occurred at roughly the same time and paralleled the emergence of 'youth culture. rock stars commanding delirious audiences.'

Fame can be traced to early acts of stage-managed achievements. Alexander the Great hit on the basic principle by taking along artists, painters, even his own historian-cum-publicist (Callisthenes) on his journeys of conquest. It was Carlyle who spotted in the 19th century how the marketplace for fame could produce heroes who were no more than celebrities with puffed-up reputations. The stage-management persists but now in a form mediated by 'consumer capitalism and a media technology adept at the reproduction of images, sounds and text.').

Potts points to the widening scope of the notion of charisma to include places (Berlin); lakes (Lake Como); plays (Pinter's The Homecoming); and my favourite, a sandwich (iceberg lettuce, with dressings which 'add charisma to its crunch').

Potts is particularly critical of the self-help, unleash-your-charisma literature. He points to the inherent contradictions within the examples he selects. On one hand they remind us that charisma is special, but on the other promise that (almost) anyone can be special, and rather quickly if their advice is followed.

Do I hear an echo of Paul's warnings about false prophets?

I felt a moment of nausea to learn that a so-called 'master of charisma' had been 'brought into the House of Lords in 1999 to "inject some charisma" into the peers' speeches, to make them a "little more Clintonesque".'

Work by the North American scholars Jay Conger and Rabindra Kanungo is seen as confirming Weber's model of charisma. Potts also suggests that the transformational model of leadership of Bernard Bass helps understand Weber's proposals for the 'routinisation' or institutionalisation of charisma

Charisma is widely found in studies of political leaders. Potts examines recent towering figures from (Jack) Kennedy to Fidel Castro, Benazir Butto, Tony Blair (unprepossessing, but with mesmeric pale eyes), and Barack Obama. He confirms the generally positive tone of many such studies. He cites an article (on Obama) which warns of the dangers of 'the politics of charisma.' drawing on Jung's idea of a 'collective unconscious' which explains the power of mythology and of myth makers such as Obama (and more generally, of charismatics). This reference to the dark side of charisma can be found in the work of the influential social scientist Emile Durkheim.

In a crisp final chapter, Potts returns to the historical trajectory of the notion of charisma. He shows there has been a radical break between ancient and modern treatments. The spiritual meaning introduced by Paul was utterly reconstructed by the secular version of Weber. Or was it? Although the term may have been 'stripped of its religious meaning, it nevertheless conveys a meaning of "giftedness", shrouded in mystery…This idea has travelled 2000 years preserving its core meaning: that is, an extraordinary gift.'. This was a page-turner. A mystery wrapped up as a work of historical scholarship. I learned that charisma is a term which can be applied to our political leaders and also to an iceberg lettuce sandwich. Worth reading by anyone who wants to make any contribution to any discussion on charisma (with or without mayonnaise).

Postscript:

So, what does *A History of Charisma* tell us about Mourinho? One significant idea point runs through the pages. Contrary to popular opinion, the modern view of charisma is that it does not come without its 'dark side'. Charismatics are often found to have a management style associated with an over-inflated ego (a narcissistic style). As the leadership researchers Conger and Kanungo put it:

'Charismatic leaders have proven to be remarkable change agents able to create or reinvent entire organizations. At the same time, these leaders provide us with lessons about the greatest dangers of leadership. For example, throughout history there have been charismatic leaders concealing a shadow side as master manipulators and purveyors of evil'.

This book reminds us again of the message of an earlier post of the fate of charismatics such as José who would 'challenge the Gods by flying too close to the sun'.

Can we Learn from Brian Clough's Leadership Style?

July 18 2010

My leadership students this week chose Invictus as a book or film worth studying. Their prior admiration for Nelson Mandela was probably strengthened by the movie. Would they have voted for Brian Clough, if they had seen The Damned United, screened by the BBC this week-end?

A case can be made for studying leadership in its widest variety of forms, including the actions of dictators as well as saints. Can we learn more from studying Nelson Mandela, or Mother Teresa or Ghandi than from studying Hitler, or Stalin. And what about sporting leaders such as Brian Clough?

The Damned United, [released March 18th, 2009], concentrates on one of Clough's few managerial failures, who after less than two months managing Leeds United Football Club, was fired for a combination of bad results and an abrasive style which extended to the club's board of directors. It was rescreened by the BBC [10.30pm, BBC2, Sunday July 18th, 2010].

Brian Clough is fondly regarded in football circles nowadays, not because he was ahead of his time but because he was very much of it, despite upsetting football's authoritarian old guard with his cocky contempt for them. He would never have got away with his genius in today's world of agents and multimillionaire egos.

With copious footage, this documentary traces his rise from a dazzling young centre-forward scythed down in his prime, turned brilliant, self-assured manager, to the ruddy-faced and bloated figure he cut in his sad decline.

When the film was first released, Prof Stefan Szymanski of CASS Business School told the BBC "It was socialism if you like …You do see this idea in business sometimes. The focus was on the needs of his players. These were his frontline staff – they're the ones under the pressure, they're the ones who

deliver, so you need to meet their needs whatever it takes.
…[however] he was a very overbearing employer, incredibly
paternalistic – like Stalin and just as frightening."

Clough himself never over-analysed his management
technique:
'They tell me people have always wondered how I did it' he
once said. 'I'm told my fellow professionals and public alike
have been fascinated and puzzled and intrigued by the Clough
managerial methods and technique and would love to know my
secret. I've got news for them – so would I'.
Would Clough have made a good business leader? In one of
his teasing philosophical dialogues, Plato has Socrates ask a
similar question: 'would a military leader be a good director of a
theatrical chorus?' But in Plato's account, Socrates was too cute
to suggest that there was a simple answer to that question. ('Just
asking' he might have tweeted, three thousand years later)

Real Rage against Barcelona

April 28 2011

Meanwhile, José now in charge of Real Madrid, has added to the customary hostility between the two great Spanish clubs. Violence erupted in the first leg of the semi-final of the Champions League, and continued into the press conference. It was almost inevitable that Mourinho would get into trouble.

The game was illuminated by flashes of genius from Lionel Messi who scored two glorious goals for Barca. Real had lost the chance to reach the final, and had suffered another defeat against their bitter rivals.

During the game, Pepe the pugnacious Real central defender who was one of José's storm troopers, added a red card to his collection and left the field. His manager also was shown red and was ordered out of the official area on the touchline into the stands. Sid Lowe reported after the match for The Guardian Newspaper from Real's magnificent Bernabau Stadium. He claimed that the Barcelona board were considering action against José for remarks that could be interpreted as an accusation that EUFA had fixed the match against Real to enable Barcelona to reach the Champions League final:

'Madrid's coach accused Barcelona of wielding untouchable power in European football and said their coach, Pep Guardiola, should feel "ashamed" if he wins a competition that "yet again" is engulfed in "scandal". Barcelona also had a man sent off, their substitute goalkeeper, José Pinto, for his role in a mass brawl as the teams left the field at half-time. The incident was one of numerous flashpoints. "One day, I would like Josép Guardiola to win this competition properly.'

There are several interesting questions raised from this pitched battle masquerading as a football match. What might it teach us about the behaviour of an outstanding leader under extreme pressure to perform? What might it add to our understanding of the charismatic leadership style.? And more speculatively, what might the story suggest about the way a leader interacts with those they come into contact with, and the effect it has on the rest of us?

And Drogba Scores

May 19 2012

Against all odds, Chelsea's interim manager Roberto di Matteo has taken the club to the brink of winning the European Cup in the semi-final against the powerful Barcelona team. Captain John Terry watches from the sidelines, and Didier Drogba threatens to win or lose the game by the intensity of his commitment.

After José 's departure, a youthful Andreas Vilas Boas was taken on as coach at Chelsea. He was being tipped as a younger but less-spiky Mourinho. Roman Abramovich who was originally in favour of the appointment, rather quickly dispenses with his services. A temporary manager, former Chelsea hero Roberto di Matteo replaces him, as the indefatigable Chelsea owner considers who would be needed fulfil his dream of winning the European Cup. After uncertain progress through the group stages of the competition, Chelsea advances into the semi-finals. It is still very much a team with a core of José 's players in it, including John Terry, Didier Drogba, Frank Lampard and Ashley Cole.

The semifinal is against Barcelona. The home leg ends 1-0 to Chelsea, with Drogba scoring the only goal after what was described as one of his more theatrical displays. Barcelona have dominated and are expected to win comfortably in the return leg.

Two weeks later at the Nou Camp, Barcelona again dominate possession, and appear to be winning comfortably. Chelsea go two goals down. To make matters worse, Terry is red carded for violent conduct and will miss the final. Then Messi has a penalty chance. This time Drogba is the culprit not the rescuer. But Messi, who has a poor record of goals scored against Chelsea, misses the penalty. The game remains poised but in a pulsating struggle, Chelsea grab a goal back. Because of the away- goals system, they are winning, and seal the tie with a second goal from the previously under-performing Fernando Torres. Will Chelsea succeed without José, where they had always stumbled before?

Chelsea's Champions League Triumph

Mourinho has left Chelsea, a victim of the failure of his team to win the Champions Cup. Their new manager Roberto di Mateo has been taken on as a temporary stopgap. For the final against B\yern Munich, their inspirational captain John Terry has to watch from the stands. Their most potent goal threat Didier Drogba is as likely to concede a penalty as score a winner.

The final of the European Cup takes place in the spectacular space age bubble of the Allianz Arena (or the Schlauchboot or Inflatable Boat in Munich as it is humorously known). Allianz have coughed up a reported eight million euros a year for thirty years for the naming rights.

The illuminated external panels are brightly lit not with the famous blue and red Bayern colours but with the EUFA green and turquoise, part of the branding deal for the final. Even with that assertion of EUFA power, the location gives Bayern Munich very much home advantage at their home stadium.

The match has echoes of the European cup win by Mourinho's Internationale team against Bayern in 2010, that time at the Bernabau. Now it is Di Mateo's Chelsea, still with a large infusion of the Mourinho's players, against Bayern managed by 'Jupp' Heynckes.

The game follows the pattern of play in that earlier match. Chelsea still show the rugged counter-attacking style developed in the Mourinho era. Bayern is the more direct and attacking outfit. After eighty minutes of constant threats from Bayern, the game is still goalless by a combination of defensive heroics, good luck, good goalkeeping from Petr Cech, and a few missed chances from Bayern.

Then a deserved headed goal by Thomas Muller bring the sides level on aggregate scores. Will Chelsea be denied a first European Cup victory yet again? With minutes slipping past, Didier Drogba muscles his way into the sporting history books with a close range header.

Extra time. Nervous Chelsea fans are expecting fate to provide one further cruel twist to snatch victory away from them. It is likely to be supplied by Drogba whose goal has galvanised him into an uncontrolled rather than a guided missile.

In two minutes of laying waste to those around him, Drogba fouls Ribery in the Chelsea penalty area. He has lost the game for Chelsea. Arjen Robben steps up to administer the final blow to Chelsea's hopes.

And Cech saves.

Chelsea's torture continues. Now the fans know that fate has decreed there will be penalties. An old joke is deeply ingrained in their belief systems. When a team from England plays one from Germany it all goes down to a penalty shootout which the German team wins.

After thirty tense minutes the penalty shootout starts. Bayern move into a lead (of course, predestined.) Fans wait for the final moment of execution. Even when Chelsea creep back to 3-3 on penalties there is little hope. It is now sudden death.

Drogba steps up to take his penalty. Yes, he is destined to seal Chelsea's fate. A billionaire squints at the action, slumped in his seat. John Terry watches helplessly away from the battle, remembering his missed penalty which gave the Cup to Manchester United in another shootout. That was four years ago in Moscow, and it was after Didier Drogba had been sent off.

Drogba places the ball on the penalty spot for the kick that will win or perhaps lose the match. Looks calmly at the keeper. Steps up.

And scores.

A relieved billionaire acclaims the consummation of his dream. A manic Didier Drogba charges around the touchline. Roberto di Mateo, Chelsea's temporary manager contemplates his future.

José Mourinho: Cult Leader and Owner of a Mystic Text

June 4 2013

A TV documentary looks back over his time at Chelsea, and examines José's near-mystic powers.

In one story related in the documentary, the press cohorts were demanding something special from the special one. Mourinho's response was startling.

'You want me to name my team? I will do more than that. I will name *their* team.'

Which he did. With complete conviction. Live, to camera.

He was to be proved completely correct.

In another interview he was asked if he played chess with the media. His reply indicates the care with which his performance is planned:

'When I face the media … before or after the game, I feel it as part of the game. When I go to the press conference before the game, in my mind the game has already started. And when I go to the press conference after the game, the game has not finished yet.'

Mourinho even has a secret document, *The Book of José* written by himself. It is said that no-one except Jos knows what's in it. So secret is, it that his words will go to the grave with him. Secret, and with the whiff of the supernatural associated with sacred texts which mere mortals are not permitted to see.

After one particularly epic performance by his team, he ordered the players to commit a highly symbolic act. They returned to the field acknowledging their legions of followers. The players removed their shirts. What or who was all that about?

Another anecdote reveals the wrath of the special one if an acolyte falls short of expectations. He once publicly rebuked the Chelsea player Joe Cole for a lack of the dedication and work ethic expected of all acolytes. In a game shortly afterwards, Cole scored a magnificently-taken goal, José gestured to him in agitated fashion from the touchline. When the player approached his manager, he discovered that he was not being acclaimed for the goal, but abused for his lack of commitment to defensive duties in the build-up to the move.

The programme also examined the strained relationship between Mourinho and Roman Abramovich, billionaire owner of Chelsea FC.

The disputed territory appears to have been over the owner's wish for success both in terms of results, and in terms of style of play. While Mourinho's personality sparkled, his team failed to capture the imagination –say in the style of rivals Manchester United.

Abramovitch had taken steps to intervene more directly, acquiring support staff and two expensive players that had not been part of Mourinho's plans for the future of the club.

A psychologist explored the messages to be found in a press conference held shortly after the arrival of the two international stars Shevshenko and Ballack.

In press conferences, José's body language is distant. No eye contact left or right. The psychologist suggested a desire for 'total control', and in this instance, evidence of a discomfort in a partial loss of control.

A few weeks after the programme was broadcast, the Special One was gone. 'By mutual consent, and with great love.'

There was a lot of religious symbolism in the programme. Mourinho ducked questions about his religion, but talked a lot about the importance of love. Like a true charismatic, he seems to have worked out his own ethical philosophy. Maybe it is all written down in the book of José.

Pat Riley, Alex Ferguson and José Mourinho

July 24 2013

When Sir Alex Ferguson retired from his position as Coach of Manchester United he received many accolades for his achievements in an illustrious career. Among them was an invitation to speak at Harvard Business School. The news took me back to a case of mistaken identity when I stepped up to give a talk about the great man.

Manchester Business School executive students have been studying Sir Alex's leadership approach for some years. Thanks to our local competitive advantage, we had access to the Manchester United club and have run sessions in their excellent educational facilities. The textbook on the course at the time even had a case study about his battle for ownership of the racehorse Rock of Gibraltar.

My story starts at an open lecture at our newly opened Miami premises. While Sir Alex was more than an interesting subject for European audiences, football was not considered to have wide enough appeal for an American presentation. Could I give a talk instead about the leadership of the outstanding basketball coach, Pat Riley of Miami Heat?

It had been a piece of accidental viral advertising. The plan had been for a low-key event for Miami business people to learn about the Manchester Business School's new programmes there. To make the event more interesting, it had been suggested that the presentation should be about the leadership style of Pat Riley, legendary coach of the Basketball team Miami Heat.

My counter-suggestion was that I would be better able to talk about Sir Alex Ferguson of Manchester United, a leader about whom I knew rather more. Eventually a creative compromise was reached, and the topic would deal with the leader styles of both of the two outstanding sporting leaders. As fate decreed it, Manchester United were making a summer tour to America at the time. This was picked up mistakenly by the media rather than a talk from a Manchester Business School academic on a visit to Miami. The MBS Office started getting enquiries which turned into a flood.

Great marketing? Maybe. An unexpectedly large audience turned up, although a surplus of disappointed basketball and soccer fans was not quite what the organizers were hoping for.

I saw what had happened too late. At best this was a great opportunity to come off the substitute's bench and win over the crowd.

It sounded too close to an earlier event I had been involved in years earlier, when I had arrived as after-dinner speaker to a business audience expecting to listen to Richard Branson's thoughts about leadership. The chairman broke the news of a change of speaker:

"Ladies and gentlemen, Richard Branson could not be here this evening. But I'm sure you agree that we are fortunate instead to be able to listen to (consults notes) to our speaker (couldn't find my name) who has agreed to step in at this late moment..." The audience did not seem to agree with the chairman. They looked palpably unenthused with the unknown coming off the bench as the proposed substitute for Sir Richard. The chairman for the evening and myself were rated Public Enemies Nos 1 and 2.

I can only recall the final flutter of applause, that time. Perhaps even that because I delivered on one sensible promise, to be brief.

In Miami, the organizers had been frantically battling to deal with expectations, without wiping out the audience entirely. Maybe, I thought gloomily, I could fess up and tell the story about the time I stepped in for Richard Branson. And remember a quote I had found from Pat Riley: "You have no choices about how you lose, but you do have a choice about how you come back and prepare to win again."

The audience was polite enough, although the silence was more one suggesting confusion more than spellbound attention. I ploughed on from my notes:

'Pat Riley now of Miami Heat is a basketball coaching legend' I began. 'His leadership style bears some comparison with Sir Alex Ferguson of Manchester United Football Club. What might their careers tell us about business success?

A young man brought up in tough early circumstances goes on to become one of the all-time legends of his sport as a coach of the highest quality and a great motivator. He became known as a master of press relations, and a coiner of memorable phrases. His playing career was successful enough, but he was never regarded as in the same class as the world beaters he went on to coach and motivate. He is often described as charismatic. He was to become rich and famous beyond the expectations of his early years. His management style is regarded as abrasive although showing unexpected sensitivity to a player's emotional needs from time to time. He enjoys the good life outside his professional work.

Sir Alex Ferguson of Manchester United or Pat Riley of Miami Heat? The facts fit the public picture of both men equally well.

For the record, I have just been relating my summary of Pat Riley's career.'

I just about escaped without a football or basketball style jeer from the audience. Later, as I read through my notes I saw some parallels in my potted biographies with the story of another charismatic manager whose on-field successes are also accompanied by memorable quotes for public consumption.

Ninety percent could apply as much to José Mourinho as to Pat Riley or to Alex Ferguson. The connections between Sir Alex and José were closer than I knew at the time, as we will soon see.

Superhuman Powers

August 12 2015

Mourinho reveals his superhuman powers of diagnosing medical injuries from the touch line and rejects the decision made by Chelsea's medical officer Eva Carneiro to delay the game's progress to attend to a player she considered in need attention. The incident was to have considerable consequences and added to Mourinho's problems until his departure in December.

[Reader alert: I replicate my post written at the time. I see now that what I thought was a fine piece of ironic reporting is too close to a rather crude sarcastic jibe at a critical incident during José's time at Chelsea.]

In the first match of the new season, league champions Chelsea draw at home to Swansea City. The Chelsea goalkeeper is sent off for a rash challenge. In the press conference after the game, Chelsea manager José Mourinho criticizes Eva Carneiro the club doctor, for attending to an injured player late in the game, an action which had forced the team briefly to continue with nine players on the pitch.

He subsequently banned Dr Carneiro from the touchline in future games. Her future at Chelsea is in doubt.

For a long time, many people have suspected that the Chelsea manager has superhuman powers. He is known as The Special One, a description that he has never denied. His gifts extend to never making a poor decision requiring him to admit fallibility.

Infrequently his explanations suggest that a match strategy has not been successful, but his true followers explain this as part of his genius at taking the blame for his players' errors. Now we know the truth.

His gift is all the more remarkable in that the doctor in question, Eva Carneiro, is a highly respected medical expert and a role model for women in football. Last year she spoke at an international conference on the challenges to women in making a career without being stereotyped as ignorant of the game

Even before Mourinho banned her to prevent such foolish actions in future games, he was accused of inappropriate behaviours for pointing out the error of her ways in such a public manner.

The article by football journalist Sam Wallace writing in The Independent [Monday 9th August, 2015] typifies such ill-informed attacks on the Chelsea manager:

'It was only on Friday that Mourinho described his faith in the medical team as "complete". What has changed since then is the innocuous Facebook post from Carneiro on Sunday night in which she thanked people for their support. It appeared that these nondescript few words of gratitude had sealed Carneiro's fate and that her time at Chelsea was as good as up.

As a high-profile woman who has taken sexist abuse from opposition fans wherever she has worked Carneiro had become a pioneer in her field for women in sports medicine'.

It is time for mere mortals to acknowledge their errors. In my studies of charismatic leadership, I am aware of the evidence that charismatic leadership is often associated with narcissism and in extreme cases with megalomania. While examples of this kind of leader can be cited, I wish to make it clear that the general observation is not intended to apply to The Special One. After all, I am not a medical expert. Nor do I have special powers.

16 August 2015

The Story rumbles on. One commentator suggested that Mourinho 'has driven blindly into a public relations car crash'.

In their next match, Chelsea incurred a double injury requiring attention from their depleted medical staff. Additional on-field medical support was provided by the opposing team.

The Charismatic Reply

September 13 2015

José Mourinho deals with press questions on Chelsea's disappointing start to the 2015-2016 season with a typical charismatic response.

It is Chelsea's fifth game of the Premiership season. The champions are languishing in the bottom half of the table, already with two narrow losses. After each loss, José claims his team to have been better than their victors.

Against Everton, the evidence is clear to neutral observers. Everton outperformed and outscored their illustrious opponents. Stephen Naismith, an early substitute for Everton, scored three goals. José continues to defend himself and his team.

The six-minute interview after the match is worth examining by students of charisma and charismatic leadership.

José is very aware of the implication of Chelsea's poor start to the season. A month ago, it was widely predicted that Chelsea would be competing to retain their position as champions of the Premiership.

Chelsea is so far behind leaders Manchester City that even José admits it will be unlikely his team will end the season as champions again. However, he continues to assert that his team has never lost to a better team.

Everton, the most recent 'inferior' team, won the points but not through a superior performance he insists.

How does he explain that? He first outlines that it is not the case of any weakness on his own part. To reassure anyone who thinks otherwise, he expands on why he remains the best manager in the premier league, and the best for Chelsea.

He also wants to make it clear that Chelsea are still the best team in the league. He avoids questions about the club's failed efforts to strengthen his defence my acquiring Everton's defender John Stones. The Everton full back was outstanding today, contributing to Chelsea's loss. From the start of the interview, José appears to be completely unconcerned about the result. He wants to show his unconcern. He would like to joke about Chelsea's bad luck, he said, that could be misinterpreted.

'I am laughing but on the inside' he says. 'Everything goes against us. I have to smile; it is so ridiculous. So many people are happy at our problems. So enjoy'

The overall message is that losing is nothing to do with weaknesses in the team or in the manager.

José is right that a lot of criticism is coming his way. The broad consensus in reports of the press conference is that deluded or deceitful in his interview. Not for José the more commonly expresses explanations of other managers when their teams lose:

We lost to a better team on the day
We have a lot of injuries at present
We have had a tough set of fixtures
My plan didn't work
The players didn't execute the plan

Such confessions hint at managerial fallibility. The narcissistic side of José makes it difficult for him to suggest such possibilities.

Body Language after the Chelsea v Arsenal Battle

September 19 2015

Chelsea shakes off its poor run of results with a win at home over its great local rivals Arsenal.

The match was to be remembered for a physical battle between the volatile Diego Costa and Arsenal's defenders. Costa was roughing up Laurent Koscielny in the penalty area and appeared to play a ten-finger overture on his face following it up with a dainty arm swing.

Another defender, Gabriel Paulista, went to defend the somewhat dazed Koscielny, and was yellow carded along with Costa. As the play was restarting, Gabriel complete his retaliation by flick kicking Costa. The initiator of the fracas staggers about in wounded innocence. Gabriel has his penalty converted into a red card and is banished from the field.

Chelsea press, and in the second half score a headed goal. Arsenal continued their card collecting, and midfielder Santi Carzola suffers the same fate as Gabriel and exits after a second yellow card. The battling nine men of Chelsea are unable to stop a second Chelsea goal.

José has the unusual task this season of taking a press conference as the winning manager. There is still plenty of ammunition which could embarrass him. His captain John Terry remains on the bench. José is challenged on the style of play, and whether he does enough to control the violence in Costa's play.

I have a suspicion that José is increasingly struggling to 'win' press interviews, although it is difficult to be sure from edited clips.

The greater part of press conference is increasingly about José. Is he still 'the happy one' he claimed himself to be at the start of the Season? He says he is not unhappy and looks as if he is not unhappy as he says it. But there are other signals that suggest it is a well-contrived bit of deception.

He puckers up his face as if he has swallowed a gristly piece of meat when questions stray into off-limit areas. This happened, for example, when quizzed about his failure to strengthen his defence further by signing the promising your player John Stone from Everton. He is increasingly tetchy when, before he might have been jocular and teasing.

I note José's unusual rapid eye movements. Typically, he gazes unblinking into space. Today his eyes dart left and right as if he is making a series of calculations or retrieving a script he has rehearsed from memory.

He emphasises the great importance he puts on John Terry, whom he has increasingly side-lined. He also nominates as man of the match. He seems to absorb or deny ambiguities as if they do not exist in his reality or in the reality of listeners.

A BBC reporter considered José to have 'stretched reality' in the interview, particularly in his praise of Costa. Compare this with the body language of today's opposing manager. Arsène Wenger interacts more as if in a discussion, taking in and offering information. Wenger presents himself as all too aware of the dilemmas and ambiguities of life.

Both are responding brilliantly in a foreign language, although this adds to the uncertainties about interpreting their respective performances.

The Battle with Jürgen Klopp Begins

October 11 2015

Klopp arrives as Liverpool FC's new manager. At his first press conference he shows that his reputation as a charismatic is fully justified. He even offers a gentle but provocative joke against José Mourinho, the Premier League's charismatic in residence

The story so far. Liverpool Football Club has a proud tradition since the days it dominated English football winning multiple league and European titles. Then there was the era of Manchester United and of increasing hostility between the clubs or at least between fans and most of the players. Now backed by Russian and Emirate wealth, Chelsea and Manchester City battle for supremacy in England, with the best players and managers that money can buy. Chelsea has brought back into the fold as their manager the ultimate Charismatic, José Mourinho. Liverpool after a brief flash of promise under Brendan Rogers lose their best player Luis Suarez, and then start the 2014-15 season badly.

Something must be done. Shortly before the Merseyside Derby match with Everton, Liverpool sack Rogers in the pusillanimous modern way with a telephone call. An announcement by the club after the match suggests a replacement will soon be arriving.

Liverpool fans tend to use religious metaphors to describe the arrival of a new manager, who is hailed as their Saviour. These epiphanies are joyful, and make subsequent reality checks all the more painful. A few rumours emerge that Jürgen Klopp, one of the most exciting and charismatic international managers, will be coming to Merseyside. To add to the piquancy, José Mourinho is struggling with an even poorer start to the season by Chelsea. His witty and engaging press conferences are also going badly.

Then a few days later. An announcement. It is true. He is coming! Klopp's captivating smile arrives in Liverpool, shortly followed by the great bespectacled one himself.

His first Press Conference is an outstanding success. Klopp captivates fans and journalists alike. Maybe the journalists are waiting for a replacement in their affections for the increasingly petulant Mourinho. The Telegraph thinks so: 'Liverpool manager dazzles on his first appearance since being appointed as manager at Anfield' it burbles.

Klopp's vision is clearly and excitingly articulated. Given time, but not all that time, under his leadership Liverpool will become great again. His grasp of English is impressive, this and his accent are additional assets. His humour is self-effacing.

He adds one little piece of mischief which set ups future battles with Mourinho, the self-proclaimed Special One, and with the financial might of Chelsea. Klopp thinks of himself as an ordinary human being. A nice message even if likely to go unheeded. Yes, he added with great timing, not special at all. Maybe you can think of me as the Normal One.

The battle lines with José have been drawn up. My *Leaders We Deserve* blog has a candidate for charismatic leader of the month.

Man, Superman and Superwoman

November 6 2015

Christiano Ronaldo says he is best footballer in the world; Serena says she is Superwoman. We take a look at the statements from self-esteem and branding perspectives.

This week, Christiano Ronaldo announced he was the greatest football player of his era. Serena Williams thwarted the theft of her mobile phone and then compared herself with Superwoman.

Together with the self-obsessed comments of José Mourinho, the stories raise interesting questions about the fragile egos of some of our sporting heroes and heroines

The apparent decline in the fortunes of Chelsea Football Club has been accompanied over several months by a remarkable series of outbursts by José Mourinho, the self-styled Special one. This week his doting fans at Chelsea roared support as his team won their mid-week Champions League match. His agent has also come to his defence as José continues to make headlines with interviewers in which he appears to be increasingly self-deluded. He has most recently lost his appeal against a £50,000 fine and a different punishment of a stadium ban.

Christiano Ronaldo who is currently playing for Real Madrid is widely regarded as one of the two top players of football playing today, along with Lionel Messi, who plays for Real's bitterest rivals, Barcelona. This week in an interview with the BBC Ronaldo makes the claim that he is the greatest football player in the world.

On the Day Ronaldo made his claim for sporting greatness, Serena hit the headlines when a very misguided person attempted to steal her mobile phone. I personally would prefer to snatch his World Cup winners medal from the great New Zealand forward Richie McCaw.

I will let Serena tell the story in her own words

'Yesterday at dinner the craziest thing happened to me. A man grabbed my phone and swiftly left.

Not thinking, I reacted (hence the superwoman photo), I jumped up, weaved my way in and out of the cosy restaurant (leaping over a chair or two) and chased him down I was too fast and was upon him in a flash. In the most menacing, yet calm, no-nonsense voice I could muster, I kindly asked him if he "'accidentally'" took the wrong phone. He stumbled on his words, probably not expecting this to happen. Eventually he said: "'Gosh, you know what, I did! It was so confusing in there. I must have grabbed the wrong phone."

This is a win for the ladies and showed every man in there I can stand up to bullies'

I wonder whether this as a rather pointless debate? Serena Williams is considered the greatest female player of her era.

Ronaldo admits that he rates himself as the greatest player of his day although others may disagree. Mourinho began the new season with an unaccustomed burst of modesty in which he indicated he no longer wanted to be considered the special one. The more this is up for debate, the harder he tries to reclaim the self-imposed title. Some might argue that any further debate is arguably pointless.

The leadership question. Is it coincidence that Serena failed in her attempt to win her Serena Slam (winning all four Open championships in the calendar year 2015) at the US Open in September? Or that José has lost much of his aura of managerial supremacy? Or that those who vote on such things continue to award Messi the accolade of football player of the year rather than Ronaldo?

The media hype angle: It is often said that celebrities collude with the media in creating and sustaining their images. Ronaldo is keen to give an interview with an interesting story in it on the week before his film Ronaldo appears on pubic release on November 9 2015.

'Prepare to Lose'

November 12 2015

Book Review of 'The Special One: The Secret World of José Mourinho'

The book was written at a time when José was re-establishing himself through the progress being made during his second period at Chelsea. Its subsequent publication in England was treated with anger and contempt from the Chelsea faithful. Even reviewers were cautious in their evaluation of the accuracy of the claims the book made.

In the spirit of a work of fiction, this book begins with a bang. The first paragraph describes vividly how Super coach José Mourinho broke down uncontrollably, one morning in May 2013, on learning he would not become the next Manchester United Manager.

José Torres, author of The Special One is a well-respected Spanish journalist, and should not be confused with a former Chelsea forward Fernando Torres, who might also have been included in such a biographic work.

If the book is essentially more fact than fiction, it undermines Mourinho's repeated claims of his unwavering love of Chelsea Football Club.

This and other claims are open to the objection that they would hardly meet the Wikipedia criteria for credibility (two citations of credible published sources per claim). The author does not include a list of references, although he does indicate in the text where these references may be sought.

Prepare to Lose is the English translation of the original title of the book. The chapter with the same title makes another sensational claim, that Mourinho conceived a bizarre plan when coach for Real Madrid. This required his team to play for a deliberate loss against Barcelona as part of a longer term plan to draw attention to injustices visited on Real Madrid.

Mourinho allegedly explained to his players would enable him to justify his repeated claims of widespread conspiracy against Real by EUFA, including scheduling arrangements and referees influenced by FIFA to make decisions biased against Real.

For readers unfamiliar with world football, when José was coach at Real Madrid, Barca was replacing then as the top team in Spain, and perhaps in Europe. Pep Guadiola was being talked of as the best coach, and Messi as the greatest player in Europe, perhaps the world. This world-view was increasingly one of the stories disputed by José in his post-match press conferences.

If there were a 'plot' against him by the footballing authorities, Mourinho's plan to deal with it is presented as a baffling and irrational fantasy. The team would prepare for a match with Barcelona to lose (hence the title of the Spanish version of book) so that Mourinho could then in a press conference, using his exceptional rhetorical skills, unveil the dastardly plotting against the club.

The author of the book might be making up a malicious calumny against José. Or he might be reporting a leaked version of what actually took place.

Did José order his players to prepare for a game which he wanted to lose? Are the claims invented? In the review mentioned above, the reviewer remained ambivalent, urging readers to decide for themselves. At very least, his press conferences recently are consistent to those described in the book in their repeated reference to enemies of Chelsea and himself; and in particular to referees and football officials. Reliable or not, this is a good read. There is plenty of evidence that the author knows his football, and writes convincingly about on-field action. His accounts of Mourinho's behaviours are mostly self-consistent and plausible. They fit accounts of a 'pure' Charismatic type so brilliantly described many years ago by Weber and more recently by John Potts (also reviewed in these pages).

And there I would have left it, a good ol' damning with faint praise review of the book. Except for a viewing of the biopic Steve Jobs on the day after I finished reading The Special One.

In the movie, Michael Fassbender gives a chilling portrayal of the great designer, visionary, and entrepreneur. As portrayed,

Jobs comes across as brilliant, self-obsessed and ruthless. it makes a convincing description of the pure charismatic type.

So much so, that we left the less than Apple perfect modernity of the Cinema complex discussing the similarities between the film of Steve Jobs, and the book about José Mourinho. The question for me might have been transmuted into a chant from the football terraces:

Are you Stevie Jobs,
Are you Stevie Jobs,
Are you Steve Jobs in Disguise?

Pity *The Special One* book did not fit snugly into my pocket. Stevie Jobs would have designed it differently, and without sharp edges.

José Mourinho has a Long Memory

November 23 2015

José Mourinho arrives in Israel for Chelsea's European Cup match against Maccabi Tel Aviv. Last year, Chelsea would have been expected to win the match easily against the weakest team in their pool. But their early season form has remained fragile. In the pre-match press conference, José remembers how Grahame Le Saux let him down fourteen years earlier.

Across Europe this week, football has been demonstrating its solidarity with the victims of the Paris terrorist atrocities. Security alerts are at the highest level. Here in Israel, there are also considerable security precautions after recent lethal attacks by Palestinians in Tel Aviv and the West Bank.

There are parallels with a match played in Israel just a month after the twin towers attack in New York in 2001. Chelsea was involved in that match too. Security concerns were so high that the European football authorities EUFA granted permission for Chelsea players to decline to play. Six players took up this offer.

When asked about security arrangements this week, José had a typically well-prepared answer.

'I didn't have a single problem within the squad. I didn't have a Graeme Le Saux. I had everybody without fears, just wanting to come. Leave security questions to people who know more than we do, and people who can do things we can't do. We just focus on playing. I didn't have a single problem within the squad. I had even a player, maybe, whose wife is going to have a baby either tomorrow or the next day but he's here, focusing on what he can do for us. So we're here focusing on getting a result. We need that for our happiness, our pride, and the people who support us.'

Why the mention of Grahame Le Saux? He was one on the six players who had declined to play in the earlier match.

Why was only Le Saux mentioned? It is a good rhetorical device to personalize a complex problem. Shakespeare shows how it is done in various stirring speeches, including the wonderful battle cry by Henry V before Agincourt. Or maybe it is an example of the way a leader might secure the commitment of the good guys by identifying their shared common enemy within the social group (Note to students: look up Leader Member Exchange theory).

There is a third possibility. The former defender is now a member of the Football Association's inclusion advisory board. Mourinho has been castigated by Le Saux for his treatment of former Chelsea medical head Dr Eva Carneiro, who is now in dispute over her dismissal from the club earlier in the year.

In the dying moments of a match against Swansea City, Dr Carneiro and Chelsea physio Jon Hearn went on the pitch to treat a Chelsea player. In Mourinho's view he was not in need of medical attention. He called their actions "impulsive and naive".

In one phrase, Mourinho was able to portray Le Saux as having demonstrated his unworthiness and disloyalty, to his club in that earlier match in Tel Aviv fourteen years earlier.

Le Saux expressed his views equally robustly:

'As someone who was privileged to play for Chelsea for 12 years, I'm saddened that it has come to this. If what started out as a straightforward employer-employee issue had been handled differently, these negative issues would not have arisen. The biggest disappointment for me is that Mourinho doesn't seem to have reflected on the damage he has done to his own image, the reputation of the club and, more important, the reputation of the entire game.'

Who's a Pretty Boy then?

December 7 2015

Trudeau sweeps to power in Canada not unaided by his sex appeal. This is a leadership idea that dares not speak its name. It may explain some of the advantages of many charismatic leaders, including José Mourinho, although it under-estimates a flaw in the 'attractiveness hypothesis'.

Are you going to write about Justin Trudeau, a Canadian friend asked me? Er, yes. How could I not? His successful campaign to become Prime minister of his country deserved more serious treatment than it received outside Canada.

I was preoccupied more with the drama of José Mourinho which seemed to be approaching the endgame. I then realized that aspects of the Trudeau case may have had relevance in explaining José's head- start in life too.

Trudeau's rise to the top is hardly surprising. He was born on Christmas Day, 1971, the son of the then Prime Minister of Canada, Pierre Trudeau, himself a charismatic and reforming leader. But like José, Trudeau was making headlines for reasons unconnected with his professional life. Even when it did make headlines, they tended to emphasize his pulchritude as much as his politics.

Is physical attractiveness influential in a leader's career? Without doubt, according to leadership experts. But the research seems rather embarrassing for those of a rationalistic way of looking at business.

During the run up to Trudeau's election success, the BBC programme Politics Today turned its attention to the issue of leadership attractiveness. Its craggy presenter Andrew Neil sustained a mood of amused detachment over the importance attributed to the physical attractiveness of leaders. To explore the case, the programme included contributions from the social commentator Peter York, pollster Katherine Peacock, and former Greek finance minister Yanis Varoufakis

Varoufakis had been included after the attention he gained as a celebrity politician as he battled with European Union leaders over the future of the Greek Economy. In the BBC studio, he even outshone commentator Andrew Neil in his expression of amused detachment, side-stepping accusations of his own celebrity status.

The programme pointed out examples of the way that unattractive political figures may be rejected at the polls on the grounds of their not being leadership material. In the UK, Ed Miliband, the former leader of the Labour party consistently received negative reviews for his appearance and his public speaking style. It all made Ed an easy target for his many political opponents. This may have contributed the surprising General Election defeat of his party in May of this year.

There was general agreement by the panel about the attractiveness hypothesis. However, Peacock added a caveat that female leaders can be 'too attractive' for their long-term success. This may be taking us into the territory of the dumb blond stereotype, often cited in feminist theory as an example of the objectifying the female form. Trudeau may be the recipient of the male version of the dumb blond stereotyping. A thoughtful exploration in The Huffington Post recently argues that he too has been objectified in a similar sort of way as a 'hot' politician.

Researchers at Aston University have looked carefully at leader attractiveness and asymmetry of features. One of their studies, published in the Harvard Business Review, starts with the attractiveness hypothesis, and the substantial evidence that physical attractiveness increases an individual's chances of being seen as and of becoming a leader.

The widely-held assumption turns out to overlook an important point. Less good-looking leaders have to work harder to gain social approval, and may as a result be better at developing inter-personal skills.

Dr Carl Senior, who led the study, explained to the Daily Telegraph 'A lot of positive social traits are attributed to symmetrical looking people. When they are growing up, everyone views them in a positive light. If you are a symmetrical-looking man you appear a more dominant, attractive individual so society assumes that to be the case'.

José Departs: Reflections on Perceptions versus Reality

December 17 2015

Leaders We Deserve subscriber Paul Hinks reflects on the departure of José Mourinho 'by mutual agreement' from Chelsea Football club

For the second time in recent history, Chelsea Football Club have parted company with their most successful manager of all time: José Mourinho. The leadership style of the self-proclaimed Special One invites closer inspection.

Mourinho has often been referred to as charismatic – but what happens when charisma is not enough? When a leader fails to take others with them?

By the time Mourinho left Chelsea "by mutual agreement" on Thursday, 17 December, 2015, Chelsea were just above the Premier League relegation zone. They had lost 9 games already in their latest campaign, compared with just 3 games in the whole of the previous season.

This was not the form of a team capable of successfully defending their title – indeed this was unchartered territory for Chelsea who had previously successfully challenged for both domestic and European honours under the ownership and guidance of Russian Oligarch Roman Abramovich. Chelsea's lowly position in the Premiership table was unexpected. Most commentators struggled to explain how a squad of players could falter so spectacularly in such a short period of time.

José Mourinho's reputation precedes him. He is a world class football coach who's consistently delivered success at some of the world's top football clubs.

This track record of success at different clubs provides some evidence to help validate widely-held opinion that 'José' is the 'Special One' – a man with some 'magic mystical ingredient' that helps him delivers success.

With the big stage comes the big personalities and the challenge of managing big player egos – the dilemmas associated with player self-interest and hidden agendas – players and their agents who may want to engineer a lucrative transfer to another club to invoke lucrative sign-on fees? Then there are the footballers' wives and partners who would prefer to shop and live in a more cosmopolitan and glamorous city. José tended to select clubs in Europe's most fashionable locations

Speculation and rumours of tensions in the Chelsea dressing room suggest José has had serious difficulties this season. The tipping point was the defeat that Mourinho and Chelsea suffered playing away to unlikely Premiership leaders Leicester City.

The Daily Mail provided further insight after the match, and days before José was to leave Chelsea.:

'When José Mourinho returns to work on Wednesday, he will be confronted by a group of grumbling Chelsea players who are far from happy with his scathing post-match analysis at Leicester City. Mourinho's use of the word 'betrayal' to describe John Terry and Kurt Zouma's defensive lapse when Jamie Vardy scored in the 34th minute at the King Power Stadium stripped the dressing room of its dignity. He has lost these players now, destroying their self-esteem in his criticism of the champions, either publicly or privately. It is a toxic dressing room now.'

Mourinho's standards are high. He expects the best from his players. During press conferences he has previously referred to his team and its members as 'Champions'. An example of how Mourinho's emotional intelligence is always engaged. When things aren't going so well, Mourinho's style falters. Inquiry and speculation starts into to what has gone wrong with the Special One's charismatic ways?

I would suggest that José 's very public clash with Dr Eva Carneiro was a critical moment in Chelsea's season and a good starting point for analysis.

The incident occurred when the Chelsea doctor rushed on to the pitch to treat an injured Chelsea player (Eden Hazzard) in the match against Swansea on 8th August.

Dr Carneiro left Chelsea FC, and the damage was done. Mourinho's misjudgement and mishandling of a single event was a pivotal moment in his recent period in charge of Chelsea.

What next for José? Mourinho's teams have consistently delivered success in silverware, the currency that fans and owners of football clubs crave for most. Mourinho is a successful football coach in commercial terms.

However, with continued success comes the increased weight of expectation. On closer inspection, José also can be seen to leave behind a less than healthy legacy in human terms.

But the signs are that José may be out, but certainly not finished. The words of another charismatic come to mind. 'I'll be back'.

Annus Horribilis

August-December 2015

The critical incidents described in the previous posts hint at the speed at which the José's successes in the 2014-2015 were followed by a descent into an annus horribilis and his eventual departure for the second time from Chelsea. I had begun began taking daily notes of the unfolding drama from the start of the season.

August 2015

A pre-season tournament had been arranged with a mysterious and exhausting sequence of matches around the world.

It proved to be a disaster for Chelsea, who were to finish without a single win. Worse, the tournament overlapped with the start of the 2015-2016 Premiership season.

Before the completion of the tournament, Chelsea was also scheduled to play a match between themselves as the previous season's league champions and Arsenal, as winners of the Capital One League Cup (still informally known as the FA Cup).

As a trophy-bearing event at Wembley Stadium, this was far from a friendly warm up for the coming season.

Chelsea continued to stumble through per-season, losing a closely contested game. This was all the sweeter for the opposing Arsenal Manager Arsène Wenger, who had been the butt of Mourinho's barbs from earlier ill-tempered exchanges. His pleasure was all the greater as he had never won a competitive match before against Mourinho, in thirteen attempts.

Their fatiguing pre-season tour had resulted in a Chelsea team that had failed to reach full conditioning.

The very first league game of the new season continued to provide evidence of the unexpected frailty of the team. It was also to produce the first serious and damaging incident of the season for Mourinho.

Chelsea's opponents were given little chance against the champions. But neither team had reached peak performance levels. A close game swung one way then another. Then Swansea equalised with a few minutes left. Mourinho was incandescent in urging his players on.

As the minutes ticked away Swansea struggled to repulse Chelsea's attacks. Then Eden Hazard fell to the ground, and the referee halted play for an injury break.

Chelsea's much respected medical doctor Eva Carneiro rushed to attend to the player, accompanied by another member of the medical staff.

From the touchline, Mourinho was screaming for Hazard to get up and get on with the game, and for the medical staff to get off the field of play. Carneiro ignored the manager and the medical break continued. Mourinho was all too aware that time would be lost on the re-start, and Hazard would have to wait on the touchline to be recalled to action.

The game petered out long before Mourinho's anger subsided. Swansea had grabbed a draw; Chelsea had lost two of the expected three home points a win would have earned.

Mourinho swiftly and unwisely put in place the dismissal of Eva Carneiro, to widespread hostile reactions. Her treatment was said to have upset the players and infuriated Dasha Zhukova, the wife of Chelsea Owner Roman Abramovich and a close friend of Carneiro.

The episode was repeatedly referred to as results worsened over the first month of the Campaign/ José continued to handle press conferences with calm reassurances that it was nothing but a blip as a result of with good fortune going to inferior teams.

His fans had previously been gorged with success since the arrival of Abramovich, accompanied by his bank balance. They remained faithful and puzzled by the bad luck visited on their team.

August stats:

August 3: The Community Shield. Arsenal 1 Chelsea 0 [*Ouch*]
August 5: Chelsea 0 Fiorentina 1 [*Mama Mia*]
August 8: Chelsea 2 Swansea 2 Exit Dr Carneiro [*Ugh*]
August 16: Manchester City 3 Chelsea 0 [*Stoppit*]

August 23: West Bromwich Albion 2 Chelsea 3 [A win! *'We are, we are, we are the Chelsea boys!]*
August 29 Chelsea: 1 Crystal Palace 2 *[Arghhhh]*

League Table at month end:
Played 4 Won 1 Drawn 1 Lost 2 Points 4

September 2015

Into September. A new month, a fresh start. Things can only get better. They did. From Horrendous results Chelsea stumbled to Not Quite So Horrendous results.

As an optimistic fan might have put it, 'we only lost one match in September, and we had our revenge over Arsenal in the league and reversed the August goals for and against ratio.'

The footballing balance sheet began to look a little better after big wins against Maccabi Tel Aviv in the Champions League and against Walsall in the League Cup (Capital One Cup).

More pessimistic fans noticed that September was passing with no improvement to the uncomfortable Premier league position of 15th. This is a few places above the relegation zone, one never plumbed before by Chelsea.

José is finding it increasingly difficult to find plausible explanations which do not imply that he might be contributing to the decline.

He is reluctant to weaken his long-established reputation not just as The Special One but as The Nearly Infallible One.

September 29 2015

Chelsea lose to Mourinho's old club Porto in the European cup. After the weekend's lacklustre performance by his club against Newcastle, he describes this as much improved, and claims the loss was down to two (defensive) moments of madness.

Costa is still out with a red card ban for Premier League matches, but was their best player in Europe.

Mourinho has continued to leave Terry out of his side. Hazard was also benched. The manager says he has no problems with the performance except for those two moments of madness. He expects to win through from the group stage of the European cup.

September stats:
September 12: Everton 3 Chelsea 1
September 16: Champions League. Chelsea 4 Maccabi Tel-Aviv 0
September 19: Chelsea 2 Arsenal 0
September 23: Capital One Cup. Walsall 1 Chelsea 4
September 26: Newcastle 2 Chelsea 2
September 29: Champions League. Porto 2 Chelsea 1
League Table at month end:
Played 7 Won 2 Drawn 2 Lost 3 Points 8

October 2015

In August the miserable results can no longer be put down to poor conditioning of players after the pre-season touring.

The stars of last year's campaign such as Hazard are not performing as well as last season. The expensive incomers are taking longer than expected to fit into the team.

For optimists among Chelsea's supports this is no more than a blip that would end, probably sooner rather than later. What goes down must come back up, so to speak.

Good players don't become bad overnight, as another pundit put it. Unfortunately, October's results were to be worse than those of the marginally better ones of September, and were back to the nightmarish levels of August.

October 2 2015

Remarkable and sad interview for Sky Sport by José after another humiliating home defeat of Chelsea. He only takes one question which invites his reactions. He supplies one long emotional seven-minute answer in which José poured out his bitterness and resentment.

He begins by talking about referees fearing to give penalties to Chelsea in Premiership matches, but also in Europe. Today he sees one such incident and the team, being in such a low position collapses.

Not clear if he refers to being low psychologically or low in league position, although I took it mean psychologically.

Then he moves on disjointedly about being sacked but will never resign. Sack me if you will, but I am the best manager he says.

This is beyond normal behaviour. Sky commentator Jamie Rednapp without malice suggested José's head was 'full of broken biscuits'. Mourinho is at best in a highly emotional state.

Post analysis shows the incident to Falcao was a penalty although decision not helped by player diving excessively. also, at least two penalties should have been awarded to Southampton according to BBC Match of the Day pundits.

October stats:

October 3: Chelsea 1 Southampton 3
October 17: Chelsea 2 Aston Villa 0
October 20: Champions League. Dynamo Kyiv 0 Chelsea 0
October 24: West Ham 2 Chelsea 1
October 27: Capital One Cup. Stoke City 1 Chelsea 1 (Stoke wins 5-4 on penalties)
October 31: Chelsea 1 Liverpool 3

League Table at month end:
Played 11 Won 3 Drawn 2 Lost 6 Points11

November

If José were a company, his balance sheets suggest he is close to going into receivership. Overheard in the coffee shop of a business school, a parody of Monty Python's dead parrot speech:

'This is a dead company. A zombie company. Deceased. Passed on. It's expired and gone to meet its maker! It's survival instincts are no more. The metabolic processes are now 'istory! THIS IS AN EX-CHELSEA BLUE'

Chelsea have now suffered three months of wretched results. José has raged against perceived poor refereeing decisions, players who were dropped for loss of form, various other injustices against himself and Chelsea

He has been increasingly easy to goad to provide an intemperate remark, which he rarely failed to do. One outburst was deemed worthy of another sanction from the FA. Its report noted José's 'disappointing record of misconduct' since returning to the UK in 2013 which had resulted in four different incidents for each of which the change against him was upheld and escalating fines and touch-line bans imposed.

November 19 2015

Chelsea play struggling Norwich over the weekend. This would be a routine win a year ago. But this season, each match is now seen as a potential show-stopper for José's second period as Chelsea manager.

Each weekend of the league season, the former England and Liverpool defender Mark Laurensen predicts results of all premiership matches for the BBC website. His own predictions show he continues to anticipate incorrectly the revival of Chelsea's fortunes. This weekend Lauro expresses the hope that Mourinho will have 'recuperated' enough to 'help him restore his state of mind, as he has not been himself' for most of the season. It is one of the very few remarks expressed publically suggesting that Mourinho's psychological condition may be contributing to Chelsea's terrible run of results.

Before the Norwich match, says he does not need more or different players in the January transfer window. He and the current squad will 'fulfil trust' placed in them by the club's owner.

November 21 2015

Chelsea just about scrape a win in 1-0 result. Maybe it is relief, but José is calmer in the post-match press conference.

'Only Tom Cruise could help Chelsea win title' one headline puts it. José is telling it as it is, showing he has not completely lost his sense of ironic humour.

November 29 2015

The latest player to fall out big time with the manager has been Costa. Their mutual disenchantment became public during Chelsea's successful mid-week European Match in Israel. Chelsea won the match comfortably, a welcome relief under its current circumstances.

November stats:

November 4: Champions League. Chelsea 2 Dynamo Kyiv 1
November 7: Stoke City 1 Chelsea 0
November 21: Chelsea 1 Norwich City 0
November 24: Champions League. Maccabi Tel-Aviv 0 Chelsea 4
November 29: Tottenham Hotspur 0 Chelsea 0

End of month League Results:
Played 14 Won 4 Drawn 3 Lost 7 Points 15

December 2015

As December starts. stories about José are now being reported discussing when not if he will go, and at which high-profile club he will re-emerge as manager. José's annus horribilis is surely drawing to an end.

Among his off-field problems is dealing with his captain John Terry who has played such a big part in José's successes at Chelsea in recent years. This year Mourinho has relegated Terry to the substitute's bench this season.

This possible rift between coach and captain had been detected as early as the beginning of October, his reinstatement not even taking place after Chelsea's horrendous run of results that followed, including defensive lapses from his promising but inexperienced replacements.

A parallel was being drawn between Mourinho's benching of Iker Casillas during his time at Real Madrid. In the book The Special One, the treatment of Casillas was considered part of a power struggle between coach and the Real captain, who was an influential leader of the team and the iconic goalkeeper of Spain's national squad.

Press reports raise the question whether John Terry's treatment may not be entirely for footballing reasons. The Independent reported on a press conference:

'When asked before the game about Terry's occasional role, and how he [Mourinho] dropped Iker Casillas when Real Madrid coach in 2013, Mourinho said the reasons were purely sporting. "Every time a big player is not playing [the media] have to try to find more than just a football reason for it... Many, many times it is just a football reason."

But it is difficult to avoid the feeling that the relationship between Terry and Mourinho has cooled. The footballing case for his continued exclusion is not obvious.

Jason Cundy, the former Chelsea defender and close friend of Terry, suggested there was a personal or political element to recent events. "If you're going to drop him, that's fine, it happens in football, but I think Mourinho is sending out a message," he said on Talk Sport. "John Terry hasn't played badly this season and I think he's been really unfairly treated. I don't think he's played badly enough for him to be on the bench."

December 1 2015

Midfielder Kevin de Bruyne's performances at Manchester City show he has been a great buy. He is among their successes of the new season with goals and assists. Mourinho had released de Bruyne as surplus to his requirements to Wolfsburg who then quickly accepted a juicy offer of £54 million from the Manchester Club to return to torment the other teams in the Premier League.

December 2 2015

José's failure to revive Chelsea's fortunes are being contrasted with the recovery of Liverpool in a 1-6 victory over Southampton. To add to José's discomfort, Liverpool's new manager Klopp is hailed as a 'magician' and the new charismatic Special One of the Premier League

December 4 2015

Gary Neville moves from football punditry to Valencia as a very inexperienced interim coach. He joins his brother Phil there, also a very inexperienced deputy coach.

Such stories are more interesting if they can be linked to José 's departure from Chelsea. This one is embellished by reports that owner Lim is aware of Mourinho's possible availability at end of season to replace Neville.

There is another festive tale which José could have done without. The players have organized a club party.

Rarely a good idea. It gives players chance to rebel or just remind others that they are not children (by behaving in childlike ways?). It is almost a sporting cliché that the press will find a boys behaving badly story involving one or more of star players involved with, shock horror, someone other than his legal or allocated WAG ('Wife or girlfriend' as the snigger terminology puts it).

The Chelsea partying seemed relatively innocuous but the press singled out striker Diego Costa for excessive enthusiasm for the full-body participation in all-night recreational partying.

Another embellishment. The volatile Costa is the most recent target of Mourinho's displeasure. He has sulked during his time on the naughty chair in contrast to the more loyal Terry.

Costa's latest display of petulance towards his manager was during the Maccabi match in was what is described as a 'bib throwing incident' when recalled to the bench from the playing field.

Mourinho decided to deal with subsequent press enquiries about the party in a manner to preserve his dignity.

Yes, he assured the questioner, it had all been fully sanctioned, and had produced useful team bonding. He suggested there might have been less than perfect bonding in the past, partly because of Costa's difficulties with the basics of English.

December 5 2015

Prior to Chelsea's home match against Bournemouth, the rumours resurface that Mourinho will take over at Valencia after Gary Neville's short term appointment there. José again bushes aside such gossip.

The champions face plucky but struggling and newly-promoted Bournemouth. Even with this season's poor start, Chelsea are expected to have relatively easy game.

Costa is experiencing further bonding with the other Chelsea substitutes.

Out on the field, Bournemouth contest valiantly. Chelsea are unfortunate when they are denied a penalty. Then in an all too familiar pattern of play, Bournemouth score and snatch the game.

Interviewed afterwards. José is unnaturally calm. He seems less agitated, more realistic. He Spends time, unprompted, saying that Chelsea is in no danger of relegation.

Now he adjusts his expectations for the season to a top six finish. This is quite remarkable and deeply disheartening to fans, the manager, the club, and its wealthy owner who was photographed in despair during the match, head in hands.

December 6 2015

Klopp's Liverpool suffer their first setback after his appointment. A disappointed Klopp in interview is all authentic discomfort, but he acknowledges Liverpool did not play well enough. Unlike José he does not comment about an incorrect offside decision which deprived them of a goal.

December 11 2015

The one bright part of the season for Chelsea is excellent progress in Europe. Today there is a 2-0 win over Porto, the team José managed in his annus mirabilis.

The press reports are treating the performance as part of a great escape for José. The performance was higher in energy, as Chelsea tops its group. Roman applauds from box (phew!), José dynamic on touch line throughout. Team likewise on pitch, no more so than the re-instated and now fully-bonded Costa (No, I can't visualise what a fully-bonded Costa looks like either).

Sky Sport notes that during the tie, support for José 'rang out from all corners of Stanford Bridge

After the match, Mourinho talks positively of Chelsea's chances of progressing in the Champions League. He mentions the efforts he made to avoid the referee's punishment by ensuring his team arrived on time for second half kick-off. Just a whiff of the old expressions of persecution? He also feels the need to report that the Chelsea owner still has complete confidence in him.

A more important match is the upcoming one this weekend against surprising premier league leaders, in-form Leicester City. Sky Bet installs the draw as most likely result (12/5. Chelsea are made slight favourites at 13/10, Leicester at 2/1).

December 12 2015

The rumours surrounding Mourinho are now spreading beyond the sports pages. The match has become billed as a make or break one for the beleaguered manager.

Terry appeared on Saturday afternoon not on the training field, but on a Sky Sports football chat show. Terry might be presumed to be surplus to requirements for the vital Leicester match.

Coveted slot as Sky pundit was vacant, because the former holder Garry Neville had unexpectedly taken up a position as coach at Valencia. It had already been rumoured that perhaps Garry was keeping the spot warm for José to take over as soon as he was released by Chelsea.

Terry was well coached at Sky in his new role. He performed as valiantly as he always did in his playing career. The show ended with a teasing question about his contribution to the upcoming match. Terry smiled weakly.

December 15 2015

I have borrowed what follows from my notes taken during the critical match against match.

Who is going to win? Pre-match, the pundits weigh-up the evidence:

"We can't believe what we see with our eyes. But they [Leicester] are top of the league, Chelsea towards the bottom, and rightly so" says Sky pundit Jamie Gallagher. He thinks Leicester will win. I am not sure.

This is it. High Noon for Mourinho.

I am surprised to see Terry is in Chelsea's starting line-up. I expected him to be still helping out Jamie at the Sky Sports control panel.

The team in white strip is playing towards the TV or West Stand end of the rapidly-filling living room. I am already in place in my favourite South Sofa end. The East sofa end is filling up rapidly.

The match starts. It takes me a minute or so to realize that it is Chelsea in their away strip who are playing in white, and it is Leicester in Royal Blue the team I thought were Chelsea in disguise.

Jamie Yardy, plucked from lower league obscurity has been Leicester's scoring sensation of the season, breaking records and opponent's hearts. His feats have obscured the skills of others in the team. The midfielder Rayid Mahrez is also outstanding.

Yardy scores slipping past Chelsea's defence as he has been doing to other teams this season and Mahrez also scores a goal.

Terry is substituted. The luckless Hazard pulls up and after an attempt to play on, signals he is unable to continue. Memories return of the first match of season when a Hazard stoppage precipitated the infamous dismissal of Eva Carneiro.

Leicester hold out after Remi closes the deficit.

Leicester manager Ranieri, always a bundle of displayed emotions, is uncontrollable. His curious embrace with Mourinho is caught on camera. There is no warmth from either side. Ranieri jerks his head away like a boxer avoiding a punch.

In the post-match interview my immediate notes resemble more detailed accounts to be found in the sports reports.

Mourinho: *They deserved to win. We concede two goals in an unacceptable way. My work was betrayed. Some players are not at normal level. Last season I brought them to a level beyond what they reached before. A top four position (to qualify for next year's European Champions League) is now not possible.*

The Premiership managerial sack race is now between van Gaal of Manchester United and José Mourinho. José is a marginal favourite to lose his job first.

December 16 (updated, a day later)

The headlines are in unison. Mourinho will go soon, a case of when not if. His 'betrayal' speech is seen a sort of resignation note.

Various factors are discussed, including the availability of one of the favoured replacements, Pep Guardiola.

Hazard's loss of form is suggested as being in part, due to the Carnairo incident at the start of the season. Hazard was the injured player, and is said to be feeling partly responsible, and uncomfortable about her dismissal. He may be called to give evidence at the employment tribunal.

Hazard's self-substitution at Leicester on Monday with an unspecified injury was among the catalogue of player actions obliquely catalogued as 'betrayal' by José in the post-match tirade.

In his book The Special One author Torres describes player discontent over Mourinho's treatment of them, but there was no evidence of sustained withdrawal of efforts by players at Real. There was evidence of selection and non-selection of players criticized as being due to 'non-football reasons'. José, unprompted, was at pains to deny any truth in such a possibility.

An article in The Daily Mail critical of Mourinho's man - management skills produces a torrent of on-line comments, showing many Chelsea fans remain deeply and unconditionally loyal to José.

I had just contacted two close colleagues by email saying I expected Mourinho to go soon, maybe in weeks.

I was wrong in over-estimating the timing. His dismissal had been taking place as I was sending the messages.

Sky has assembled a panel of their available football pundits, Paul Merson, Thierry Henry, Graeme Souness and Scott Minto. All seen somewhat shocked by the news.

Paul Merson: 'Manchester United would be interested in getting José if results do not pick up'.

Thierry Henry: the players contributed to Mourinho now being out of the boat. Who is available [to replace him]? How will he bring back commitment and desire?'

Graeme Souness: 'I think a few main men gave up on him. Something fundamentally gone wrong.'

Scott Minto. 'I'm not surprised. His comments [about his betrayal] were part of his dismissal. His style is OK at first but not for the long term. He's not able to change his style.'

I mark the stunning event by stopping collecting statistics about José's annus horribilis at the moment of his dismissal.

December stats [to José 's last match as manager]

December 5: Chelsea 0 Bournemouth 1
December 9: Champions League. Chelsea 2 Porto 0
December 14: Leicester City 2 Chelsea 1
[December 17: The Sacking of José Mourinho].

José's second stay at Chelsea has come to an end.

A Helicopter Hovers over a Large Brightly-lit Building

December 17 2015

The television screen clears for a special news bulletin.
A helicopter hovers over a large brightly-lit building. There is no sign of life outside the perimeter of the premises. It is reminiscent of the scene earlier in the year of the stake-out of terrorists holed-up an industrial warehouse outside Paris.

A caption streams across the bottom of the screen. I was not looking at a military operation. The moving caption announces the breaking news: 'José Mourinho is sacked by Chelsea'
The unfolding story was to dominate sport and general news headlines for several days.

2.30 PM

I had just contacted two close colleagues by email saying I expected Mourinho to go soon, maybe in weeks. I was wrong in the timing. His dismissal was taking been taking place at around 2.00 pm, as I was composing the messages.

'Light Will Overcome Darkness'

25 December 2015

It is Christmas Day. Her Royal Highness Queen Elizabeth II presents her annual Christmas Message to her people. It is her sixty third such message, a tradition broken only once, in 1969, when the broadcast came in the form of an intimate if bland documentary of the Royal Family.

That was at a time when younger members of the extended family were much into the creative media. Such a daring break with tradition was quickly decided one step too far in demystifying the monarchy. For example, it showed rather democratic looking leftovers from the royal breakfast table being packed away in Tupperware plastic containers. Perhaps wisely, almost all records of the film have been removed from public scrutiny.

Today's message has echoes of the Queen's 'annus horribilis' speech. It has indeed been a year when news has been dominated by extremist attacks, and millions of displaced people shown through instant media transmission desperately seeking a new life, as wealthier nations juggle compassion with attempts to strengthen border controls amid fears of public disruption and social breakdown.

The Queen shared the comfort she gains from a verse from the bible:

'It is true that the world has had to confront moments of darkness this year, but the gospel of John contains a verse of great hope, often read at Christmas carol services: *The light shines in the darkness, and the darkness has not overcome it.*'

The Queen's speech is an occasion that invites each viewer to reflect on personal moments of light and darkness. After a few moments of private and public reflection, I spare a thought for José.

A week ago he was The Special One commanding the fortunes of a special football club closely associated with The Royal Borough of Chelsea and Kensington itself set the heart of the Monarchy's estates, the now appropriated Chelsea Barracks, and a few minutes' ceremonial canter to Horse Guards Parade and Buckingham Palace.

Mourinho too is reflecting somewhere on the light and darkness of his annus horribilis. I have no doubt that the story is not ended.

A moment of silence. I am still lost in my own thoughts.

From a stadium in my mind a crowd begins to sing. The words are from a hymn adapted as the Football Anthem sung before each Cup Final at Wembley stadium. The music is to the tune Eventide but better known as Abide with Me, the title and first line of the hymn. The mood of words and music match evocatively and darkly. The crowd reaches the fourth verse:

Thou on my head in early youth didst smile,
And though rebellious and perverse meanwhile,
Thou hast not left me, oft as I left Thee.
On to the close, O Lord, abide with me.

I think of José, smiled upon in youth, rebellious and perverse meanwhile. Then I wonder. Has he really left us, or have we left him?

The Magical Managerial Roundabout

Following José's departure from Chelsea, there was an unprecedented storm of media stories about his replacement. The image of musical chairs comes to mind, or maybe that of a managerial magical roundabout with players, managers, (and even owners) jumping on and off as the speed of the roundabout dictates. The lucky ones get off safely and have a better ride waiting for then. Others are pushed off without such promising prospects in view. We trace the breaking stories in the month following his removal.

There are many speculative news reports about José's own future. Like a jigsaw with a key piece of the puzzle removed, other pieces of the international managerial jigsaw have to be examined to find out where they best fit in.

Candidates for José's replacement are those top managers with the greatest track record of success. Availability is not a major consideration. The assumption is that anyone becomes available if the buying club has the resources to attract the best manager that money could buy.

This produces considerable opportunities, but also in the language of business strategist, chaotic or turbulent conditions in the marketplace.

December 17 2015

When José's departure was announced, 200,000 tweets were posted in the next few hours. An estimated forty percent were humorous. The ones I read were of the usual mix of grossness, banality, humour and sometimes brilliance.

I rather liked one about sacked Chelsea medical officer Dr Eva Careiro, 'with smile on her face, putting away her set of voodoo dolls'.

December 20 2015

Within days, speculation returned to an old story that Mourinho wanted to join Manchester United.

Why not? At that club, Louis van Gaal was failing to turn around its fortunes. As one commentator put it, if Man United really want José why not do it now or miss the opportunity.

Influential figures at the club had openly suggested he was not an ideal choice. One article indicated the concerns noting 'Mourinho and United feels like a collision, rather than a working relationship - and the conflagration could either set the rest of the Premier League aflame or just United.'

For any of several reasons, Manchester United remained cautious about snapping up José.

Media speculation was heightened by the news about the availability of Pep Guardiola. He has announced his departure from Bayern Munich, where he is to be replaced with Carlo Ancelotti, a veteran football manager with an impressive list of battle honours.

Pep is the hottest property in market at present. His track record of success is unrivalled. He has skilfully positioned himself as open to invitations for a top job in The Premier League in 2016.

After José's departure, Chelsea was an obvious possibility for Pep. Manchester United had been interested in Guardiola as a successor to Sir Alex Ferguson, but may have played their hand badly. Their noisy nouveau riche neighbours Manchester City are believed to have nearly a done deal.

Pep has the status to turn down the largest financial offer in preference for managing a club that will match his ambitions for it without undue influence from its owner and advisors.

The festive season is nearly upon us. upon us, with the prospects of managerial reshuffles postponed. In a few cases, such as Louis van Gaal, the results of the next matches may determine his future

January 3 2016

January is the period when clubs exchange players and cash with expressions of good will. It is also a time to consider other managers on the magic roundabout and whether there will be changes to be expected in the months ahead.

Chelsea, with their new caretaker manager Gus Hiddink, have played three draws since José's departure. John Terry has been reinstated alongside the raw but talented defender Zouma.

The next Premiership game is away to in-form Crystal Palace. This will be a good test of any significant improvement by Chelsea.

Fifteen minutes into the game Hazard shows some sort of groin strain. A few minutes later he indicates he can no longer continue. Mourinho hinted at his suspicions of the authenticity of Hazard's injuries, and perhaps his disloyalty since the Careiro episode in the opening game of the season. But the evidence of a persistent injury is increasing clear. A few minutes later Hazard indicates he can no longer continue. But Chelsea go on to produce their best performance since Hiddink arrived, and win 0-3.

Perhaps they have begun the painful climb back towards last season's form. The manager later talks cautiously about the possibility of achieving a top four finish to secure a Champions League place next season. If so, the club's removal of José will be seen as a successful decision. José had admitted such a goal would require a superhero.

January 4 2016

Carlo Ancelotti who replaced Pep Guardiola at Bayern Munich two weeks ago, says it is hard to understand why Real Madrid has sacked Rafa Benitez. Real has had five managers since 2009. Rafa's replacement is Zinedine Zidane, is an iconic footballer but still inexperienced as a manager.

January 6 2016

Just when Chelsea must have thought there would be fewer distracting media stories of the club and its former manager, the Eva Carneiro tribunal gets underway. She is suing the club for constructive dismissal and breach of contract.

The preliminary hearing, held in private, takes place at the London South Employment Tribunal in Croydon. There is a separate but connected legal claim against José which is a guarantee of additional media interest.

January 7 2016

It is reported today that Chelsea approached Carlo Ancelotti five weeks before sacking José. This is really magic roundabout stuff. Ancelotti was dispensed with as Chelsea manager to make way for Mourinho in 2009.

Ancelotti might still have been pragmatic enough to return under the right conditions, but didn't want a short term contract, maybe to be caretaker for Guardiola.

January 8 2016

Chelsea continues to attract press attention. A training ground spat between Diego Costa and Oscar, was worked up into a story. The two are known to be good friends. Costa retains interest as the Chelsea villain of the piece, while retaining fan loyalty for the reasons others cast him along the lines of an uncontrollable enforcer.

A more significant story is one providing financial figures which show Chelsea at the top of the league table for the first time this season. Unfortunately, their table-topping achievement is for the payments made to the club's players.

Thanks to the application of what is sometimes called creative accounting, the club evades punishment by EUFA. The process is assisted by nifty conversion of loans from Roman Abramovich into different parts of the balance sheets.

The practice is shown to be one shared by the other clubs with the resources to do so. Manchester City, Manchester United and Arsenal in the English premiership, Real Madrid and Barcelona in Spain.

January 10 2016

I discuss the movements of top managers after José's departure from Chelsea with football pundits and technical advisors Susan and Paul, who are on Mourinho watch for me.

Susan emails back 'It's like the circulation of elites...'

Nice one, Susan. Pareto does not get mentioned much by football writers although he has much to teach us about the special ones he described as elites.

Vilfredo Federico Damaso Pareto (1848 -1923) was an Italian engineer turned economist and political scientist. His work added to our understanding of the unequal distribution of wealth. His way of measuring this was extended into other fields and is known today as the Pareto ratio or the 80:20 Principle, which has been applied to many business and engineering situations. It would predict, for example, that 80% of footballers' earnings would be paid to 20% of footballers.

His theory of elites mentioned by Susan was influenced by the work of Machiavelli. Pareto presented a kind of sociological roundabout with Machiavellian foxes outwitting and being outwitted by lions.

The big tough scary members of a ruling elites are lions, the Machiavellian ones are foxes. Elites, he proposed, get on in life because they are, well, just darn superior. The elite managers are at the front of the queue for employment if a plum post becomes vacant. First on the roundabout if a place is vacated.

A somewhat distasteful philosophy for our democratic age.

It makes you think, though...

My own reading is that managers are mostly foxes, and owners often ferocious lions.

January 14 2016

Pep is particularly well aware of his position among the fox hierarchy of special ones at present. His mystic musings could come straight out of the sacred text of José.

January 16 2016

Chelsea are reported as showing interest in Diego Simione of Athletico Madrid as the future replacement as their Special One.

Another report suggests that Pep's anticipated move to Manchester City will allow Chelsea to make a successful bid for the club's current manager Manuel Pellegrini. The magic roundabout is in full swing.

January 17 2016

It is now a month since José left Chelsea. Speculation continues about his future. The special one has become the silent one.

But today a story breaks saying that José has remained in England. His self-esteem seems to have recovered from the dark days of the few months, and from those increasingly fraught press conferences spent defending the indefensible.

He is planning a return to management in the Premier League. His plan is consistent with his ambition one day to manage Manchester United, outlined so dramatically in The Special One. According to today's story, José is confident of getting the job at Old Trafford before the start of the new season. That would be approximately a year after the start of his annus horribilis.

Reader Guidance Warning

Any readers with a liking for book to have a clear ending stop here. Otherwise, you may find that what follows includes material of a disturbing and confusing kind.

A month has passed since José left Chelsea for a second time. His annus horribilis has ended.

The Queen's Christmas message to the nation talked of how light will overcome darkness, a particular consolation for Chelsea supporters still in mourning over their departed Special One. José has gone to ground, leaving the managerial roundabout to continue its dizzy orbiting without him.

What more is to be said, beyond a few appended sections for students and those who like to test themselves with quizzes?

There is one more thing. Suppose everything you have read so far is just a story? One that is plausible, and is taken for granted as true, but is no more real than a work of fiction?

If you are prepared to consider such a possibility, read on.

If not, you risk reading what might seem to you as pointless fantasies of an author who has lost his grip on reality.

So don't say you haven't been warned. If you decide to quit before the final whistle goes, I just want to say I understand. Even the most faithful fans do that from time to time.

And if so, thank you for your company up to this point, and best wishes for your future, with or without further appearances of The Special One.

Another Story about José

Still with me? Good. You are the fearless ones, willing to take on a challenge, to boldly go where few have gone before. Willing to gamble your time. You are among life's season ticket holders who never leave a match until the final whistle goes. One of the real fans. What follows is for you, willing to seek out the new, the untested and untasted, with a discerning appetite, a veritable gourmet among gourmands.

My offering comes in the form of an extended fable entitled *The Chronicles of José Mou*

A discerning reader like yourself will have suspected in a flash that José Mou is no other than José Mourinho in disguise.

'We know who you are
We know who you are
You're Mourinho in disguise.
[CLAP CLAP CLAP]
You're Mourinho in disguise.'

And you would be right.

I include it, even after the warning from a concerned friend that I do so at risk of being suspected of producing a piece of pretentious academic flummery.

This is my defence. José Mourinho's story is a made-up one anyway. All I have done in the preceding pages is assemble the story trying to make some sense of it. You could say that José constructed the story which is then picked up and discussed until some version gets accepted as the truth. For me, the story is a joint production between a leading figure in a drama and assorted other cast members.

There are other influences which go into the performance, including the audience for a play, and the readers for a book.

All this adds up to the leader's tale. That is why I like the idea that we don't just get the leaders we deserve, we invent the leaders we get.

So I have invented another tale. Its hero José Mou is a bit like the Mourinho we have encountered in these pages already. But by distancing myself somewhat from the older story, other possibilities emerge. The new story describes a series of battles, the generals involved, and the impact of the actions of the generals and others influencing the battles.

Like many other stories it is in three parts: The First Coming; Exile and Return; and Betrayal. Its hero José Mou is presented as a superhero from a galaxy far away. Maybe it is 'just a story'. Or maybe like all stories it suggests something fresh to challenge our earlier beliefs.

The Chronicles of José Mou: The First Coming

Once upon a time, in a galaxy far away, an ancient force is stirring, willing itself into life, to become a threat to the prevailing galactic powers. The fate of the rival powers lies in the hands of one special being, by the name of José Mou, who comes to life as if a mere mortal in a remote region of a small planet, where he spends his youth living a humble life among its inhabitants.

It is a time in which old rivalries are settled by fierce contests. Each territory has an army directed by a battle-tested General who swears allegiance to his liege lord or King.

The conflicts are particularly intense in the Europa region of the planet, in which the young Mu is to grow up and reveal his special powers.

As the Galactic Standard Time [GST] approaches the second Millennium, rivalry is particularly intense in the island territories of Britannia to the west of the mainland of Europa from which the great General Bobito is about to undergo a journey in which he encounters the young José Mou.

1992 GST: General Bobito, once the premier military figure in the islands of Britannia has been outmanoeuvred by inferior men with greater political skills. He moves in disgust to the Iberian territories on the mainland of Europa to seek new challenges. There he discovers the young Mou who uses his powers to translate many tongues into the English dialect which General Bobito understands, and to explain to the warriors what General Bobito commands them to do in battle.

Mou quickly becomes the General's most valued assistant. In return he teaches Mou his special military arts.

2000 GST: In Britannia the power struggles continue. Greybeard Bates, an aging but wily merchant, has become chief steward of the estates of Stamford Bridge on the banks of the river flowing through the states. He has gained this powerful position for a single bitcoin of the realm through his cunning. He recruits the wise General Claudio as his military advisor.

2002 GST: Mou, through the influence of Bobito, had been placed in charge of the military contests of the city of Porto, known for its fishing and for a fortified wine exported around the world.

He quickly shows outstanding military skills. His forces win the great CUP of CUPs which is competed for every year by all the forces of the lands of Europa. The General who wins that trophy is in great demand by the wealthiest rulers in all of Europa, including High King Bromanovich.

2004 GST: High King Bromanovich invades the Stamford Bridge territories and settles there. Greybeard Bates negotiates a handsome settlement and goes off to the Northlands in search of ways of adding to his newly acquired fortune.

The High King's advisers alert him to the special powers of Mou and his triumphs in winning the great CUP of CUPs. Bromanovich sends for the young General and welcomes him on his floating palace. José reveals a part of his secret knowledge illustrating with many a gesture charts of new ways of defeating enemies. He also reveals weaknesses he has divined in Claudio's plans for The High King's army.

The scales fall from the eyes of the High King and he decides to dismiss Claudio and replace him with Mou.

His councillors advise against his decision and warn him of the dangers of becoming involved in the dark arts practiced by Mou. The High King brushes their objections aside.

Claudio, a noble warrior, accepts his fate but vows to himself that one day the High King will regret his dismissal.

José is appointed the commander of the High King's forces, with orders to win him fame and respect to match his boundless wealth. In particular, he is charged with winning the famed CUP of CUPs, this time for the High King.

Mou pledges his undying loyalty to King Bromanovich.

2005 GST: José sets out on his quest to capture the great Cup of Cups for the High King. In his first campaign he loses a vital battle. He reacts as much in anger. Rather than weaken his army's faith in his special powers, he blames the defeat on an official of the mighty FIFA whom he accuses of favouring his opponents. When he loses another contest he repeats his accusations and becomes a sworn enemy of the twin Lords Platini and Blatini, the most powerful of the administrators of all officially sanctioned military contests on the planet.

2006 GST: José leads his army of warriors into battle against one of the most powerful forces from the Northern territory, led by Sir Alex the Rosicrucian, long hailed as the greatest General in the land. In a thrilling battle, José's men defeat the Rosicrucians and are recognised as the champions of the battlefields of Britannia south of the borders with Hibernia.

Emboldened by this victory, José asks The High King for reinforcements for his men in future battles. The High King agrees, on condition that they are to be picked by himself from among his own favourites. This angers José who unwisely shows his displeasure by holding back the promotion of the High King's favourites.

King Bromanovich remembers the warnings that José would be a threat to his authority. With a heavy heart, he decides he must strip Lord Mou of his titles, and banish him from future employment in his territories.

Mou departs, swearing his continued loyalty and support to the High King and his people of Stamford Bridge

The Chronicles of José Mou: Exile and Return

2008 GST: José moves to Europa's eastern flanks, and the romantic regions of Italy, where leadership has developed as an art through the teachings of the great military advisor Machiavelli. He takes up employment in the city of Milan to oversee the forces fighting under the name of Internationale.

José uses his special powers to train up the Internationale and begins to win battles again. Their fierce rivals La Forca are dedicated warriors of the political leader Viscount Silvio Ballastroni.

2009 GST: Under José's command, Internationale wins the cherished Cup of Cups. José's fame continues to spread. But with fame comes envy and enemies. His adversaries mount in numbers. Ballastroni induces his many allies among the Generals speak out against him. Platini and Blatini exert their baleful influence to weaken his efforts.

His opponents still taunt Mou for ignoring the romantic form of attacking combat in favour of a crab-like carapace of solid defence from which his forces would emerge having bored or exhausted the opposing army. is headstrong. He chooses not to hold his council and continues to show disrespect and contempt. His powerful enemies call for his banishment.

In England, the High King has become increasingly jealous of José's achievements in Milan. He appoints and dismisses Generals, in frustration, seeking a worthwhile replacement for José.

His latest leader is Carlo the Calm, famed for his wisdom and composure when under fire.

2010 GST: A configuration of the heavenly orbs means that José and his Internationale cohorts must go into battle against those of The High King Bromanovich to progress in the Cup of Cups

The first of the two contests takes place on the vast plains of the San Siro, the chosen battlefield of José's Internationale brigade.

José's men inflict a narrow victory on the High King's army commanded by General Carlo, but there is still all to fight for in the return contest.

This takes place in the heartland of the High King's territories at Stamford Bridge where once José had been commander in chief. Once again, José drills his men well, so that they are skilled in defence and swift in counter-attack. They gain another victory. The High King's dream of winning the Cup of Cups is over for another year.

José has defeated the High King but then loses the next contest for the Cup of Cups, and has to yield the title of greatest General in Europa, and grand victor in Cup of Cups campaign.

The loss is another blow to his pride. He is increasingly punished him by his political enemies and sickened by the plotting of his own players against him. José decides to leave Internationale.

In far-off England, there is a new force in the land bearing the banner of the Blue Moon. The army is backed by the wealth of a great potentate from the East. The skilled and well-trained army is fighting from a stronghold in the Northern territories. These skilled fighting men present another threat to the High King's ambitions. They are also said to have the resources to defeat those of the forces of Sir Alex and have cheekily struck camp a short distance from the towers of Old Trafford. José decides against returning to England until a more propitious time. He conceives the Idea of a new start in one of the great city states of Spain. He sees the progress being made there in Barcelona where he had been assistant under General Bobito. When he offered Barcelona his service he is rebuffed.

He turns to the opportunities offered in the City State of Madrid. He accepts an invitation to place himself at the service of a noble and ancient society dedicated to protecting the honour of the city. By royal assent the society is known as Real Madrid.

Real is facing from the grave threat presented by the new power emerging in the land, coming from the forces of Barcelona. José's admiration for Barcelona turns to enmity, and particularly toward its military leader General Guadiola who had been appointed there in preference to himself.

2011 GST: José's loyalty to Real was total, as was his hatred of its enemies. In the ensuing battles between Real and Barcelona no prisoners are taken. All rules of engagement are forgotten in the fray.

As happened throughout his career, José wins the affection of many of his followers. But there are to be no great triumphs, no additional wins of the Cup of Cups at Real. Worse, Barcelona, led by their General Gladiola, continue to win the major prizes in contests against José and his Real warriors.

José becomes increasingly depressed. For all his triumphs, he remains sensitive to slights about his achievements, about his unique status. At times he would lead his men passionately and directly in the heart of battle, rather than directing like a General is expected to do from above the fray. He realizes that he longs for a return to England.

2013 GST: News reaches Madrid that the great leader Sir Alex the Red of the Northern territories has retired with full military honours. José is uplifted, as he believes himself to be the chosen one to replace him. But the wily Sir Alex has been plotting against him with some of José's most bitter rivals to find his successor to compete against his new enemies fighting under the Blue Moon banner.

To his horror, José sees that he has been betrayed by the smooth words of Sir Alex, and vows to redress this wrong. He wonders whether The High King might be receptive to taking him back to Stamford Bridge and sends ambassadors for secret talks with Bromanovich.

With some reservations, Bromanovich eventually realises that he still needs José if he is to achieve his dreams. He sends an invitation to José to return.

The High King again sets conditions to protect his own power, retaining the right to reject requests from José on behalf of those he knew would become more loyal to José than to himself. José again accepts the conditions reluctantly and swears his loyalty again to the High King.

His return is greeted tumultuously by supporters still loyal to The Special One

I am now The Happy One, José declares.

2014 GST: José has lost little of his special powers in battle. He pleases the High King by defeating the forces of the Blue Moon. The successor to Alex the Rosicrucian is struggling to retain the support of the red forces and is no longer a serious threat.

2015 GST: At the end of the fighting season, with the summer break approaching José is that most fortunate of Generals being mostly successful and at times lucky. He is loved by his troops and camp followers.

The High King celebrates the victories and trophies won for him by José, but he still longs for the unfulfilled achievement of possessing the Cup of Cups that José had delivered twice to other potentates in other territories.

However, he keeps those thoughts to himself, hoping that this one last prize will soon be delivered to him by The Special One.

Discussions around the next campaign begin concerning which Generals are most likely to win the greatest victories. In Britannia, José is among them, as is the courtly but ancient warrior, Sir Argos Wellbeloved, Commander of the High Berry Fusiliers in a neighbouring territory.

Other favourites include General Pellagra of the Blue Moon army and the recently appointed General Vanerama of the Rosicrucians in the Northern territories.

General Claudio who was replaced by José on his first arrival at Stamford Bridge, is now commanding a frail army which only narrowly escapes exclusion from the premier campaign battles. He is considered favourite only for the number of humiliations he will endure in combat against the likes of José Mou's guile and his well-trained fighters.

The Chronicles of José Mou: Betrayal and Beyond

Many years of Galactic Standard Time have elapsed since José Mou arrived on planet Earth. Now time becomes compressed as ordained by the great Time Lords Doctor Who and Professor Einstein, his most famous prophet from the planet Earth.

The fate dictated for José Mou by the Time Lords unfolds ever more rapidly in the months following his Campaigns in the first half of the year 2105 GST.

As the spring campaign ends, José revels in the adulation of his supporters as he receives the cup as National Champions. He had no reason to feel other than satisfied by his achievements, fulfilling the prediction that he has returned not only as The Special One but as The Happy One.

But his outward impression of confidence conceals a concern that his troops have already given their all in the last campaign. He knows that his warriors require a longer break than usual, so exhausted are they after their efforts. They have to shake off their fatigue. He is gambling on the number of minor contests to be won before they reach total readiness for the major battles ahead.

He approaches the High King with suggestions for reinforcements.

King Bromanovich agrees with all but one. He sends for a favourite warrior from his own land in preference to a great fighter requested by Mou. He considers the proposed champion would be too loyal to Mou rather than to himself.

José sees this as a demonstration of a lack of trust, and decides to show the High King he is ill-advised to ignore his requests in such military matters.

José suspects the warrior forced on him could be reporting back to the High King. He also reflects again at the loss of fighting spirit shown by the brilliant young officer who had received personal accolades in the last campaign.

José concludes that stern measures are called for to deal with such ambitious lieutenants who are too fond of claiming the credit for their achievements, and who do not speak out in recognition of how much of their success is the result of José's methods and mentoring.

He sets out to teach them humility, knowing otherwise they would otherwise become unreliable and ignore his orders. He recalls that has always been the case, and he prepares to deal with the bad eggs, the potential trouble makers.

As was his habitual practice, he pours over intelligence reports of his protagonists in the upcoming campaigns, working long into each night, calculating, anticipating, and looking at ways of accumulating advantages.

He knows the importance of a good start in the new season. In the opening contest of he faces a courtly but ancient warrior, Sir Argos Wellbeloved, who commands the High Berry Fusiliers. His army has a long tradition of success, exceeding the historic victories of José's forces.

José takes to the offensive, belittling Sir Argos in public. They may be called The Fusiliers he joked but they always fire blanks against me. I am a master of success. Sir Argos is master only of failure and leader living on past glories.

Sir Argos refused to respond to the verbal slights hurled at him. He too had studied the intelligence reports and could see his opponents were ill-prepared for the contest.

The High Berry Fusiliers win a close tussle. José claims they he has not obtained needed reinforcements, and has lost to a fortunate attack from a weaker force.

José's gamble on the fitness of his players has failed.

"You aren't happy anymore" chanted the supporters of the Fusiliers from the outskirts of the battles.

José has little time to return his forces to fighting fitness. Next up there is a joust at Stamford Bridge against an international force but in a modest competition. However, José knows that another loss will anger The High King.

His men are still ill-prepared and lose another battle.

Once again José shrugs off the defeat saying it will be different when he faces the first important contest in the campaign for the national league title they had won a few months earlier.

José's warriors next face a force from the regions of the Wild West, ferocious fighters proclaiming themselves loyal to the memory of King Arthur and his magician Merlin.

Despite his special powers, José's fighters are unable to deal with the necromancy deployed against them. José knows his plans should be able to succeed against the old Celtic wizardry. His men continue to struggle. He screams for more effort, particularly from the young champion of the last campaign. It is too late. He falls to ground as if a victim of a mortal blow. José sees he has not been touched my any animal, vegetable or mineral object. José recognises it as a Celtic spell. José screams an incantation to rouse to stricken warrior, but then sees the cunning of his enemies. His own medical officer, the beautiful Eva, has also fallen under a spell and rushes to the field of battle to the aid of the wounded warrior.

José shouts to Eva for her to go back to her medical post. He curses her foolishness, but it is to no avail. Moments later the trumpet sounds and the fighting ceases. The armies recover their wounded men, exchange pleasantries, and apply healing portions for those still suffering from the blows or spells laid upon them.

The beautiful Eva has disobeyed his orders and costs them the victory. She must not be allowed to stay in the camp. José orders her dismissal. But Eva is much loved by his Knights for her gentleness and medical skills.

José counts the cost of removing Eva. As his troops prepare for the next contest, he hears rumours that confirm his worse suspicions. There is someone, it is whispered, has let it be known that he would rather lose than see Mou triumph. He is confirmed in his belief that there is a traitor within the ranks of his fighting men.

José's next contest is against a formidable foe, and the new force in the land, The Blue Moon army. They have built their stronghold in the Northern territories.

José knows that he will prevail if his forces show their true fighting mettle. He outlines his carefully prepared plan to defeat the Blue Moon forces.

But once again there is only bitter defeat. José sees there is more than one individual failing him in the heat of battle. All of his best fighters are holding back. He is being betrayed from the inside of his own army.

When the trumpet sounds ending the contest he has been easily beaten.

He pours all his superhuman powers into reversing his ill fortunes in the coming contests.

His speeches before battle are even more rousing. But as well as sweet words, he shows his anger against any warrior for transgressions of his fighting orders. Even the most famous of them are taken from the fray in disgrace and replaced by others. Some are sent to distant regions in what seems for trivial reasons until he José decides they are ready to return with humility and willingness.

His faithful captain and heroic defender John the Terrifying suffers José's displeasure, and spends time outside the battle lines, watching the raw recruits who had taken his place in action.

José's outbursts against the officials overseeing the contests are also becoming more frequent and intense. He accuses the highest officials of plotting against his army, and of course against himself.

He is brought before the military courts of justice, charged and found guilty of gross disrespect of their authority.

In punishment, he is forced into temporary discharge of his duties and is prevented from communicating with his army for several battles.

Weakened by these series of blows, José's men continue to lose contest after contest. He feels the humiliation of being jeered at as a spent force, the accusation he had made against general Wellbeloved. His army faces relegation to minor tournaments with paltry rewards inadequate to retain their loyalty.

José is still loved by the ordinary people faithful to the Stamford Bridge cause. As his army arrives to do battle, followers still call out his name as he passes by, and hold up banners made from bedsheets and decorated with slogans in Samford Bridge royal blue declaring their true love for him.

But whispers are whispered. There is talk that the High King will strip him of his powers as he did once before.

His last chance arrives in December as his men face the forces commanded by General Claudio. Since his dismissal by the High King and his replacement by General Mou, Claudio has retained admiration across Europa for his integrity, but his triumphs have been few compared with those achieved by the Special One.

In this season's contests, Claudio he has led his unfancied army to more victories than those gained by any other General. Even so, many observers still consider that the fighting forces commanded by Mou are superior to Claudio's troops.

The Stamford Bridge warriors start well and seem to be pressing their opponents back in defence.

But Claudio has found a way of releasing the attacking skills of his previously unrated attacking men. Two lightning fast-thrusts slice through the defensive lines. José's army is outflanked each time. The final trump sounds, and his defeated army drags weary limbs from the field of battle, often unconnected to other parts of weary bodies. The official blue cross ambulance remains unmanned, parked with the official blue cross bus adjacent to the field of battle.

José realises he must do something special or he will be destroyed as their commander in chief.

He has to prove to the world that he is as powerful as ever. It is time for his greatest speech in which he will address the world, but will also reveal the perfidy of those traitors who have deprived him of the victories he deserves.

He first pays credit to Claudio, the man he deposed those many years ago.

José then addresses his army and his special champions. He says he has been betrayed by treachery of the worse kind. He points out the traitors indicates one by one.

The High King listens, bows his head in bitter shame. He knows that José has not just been defeated, but has chosen this way to throw himself on his sword.

In defeat he has chosen the timing of his departure from employment in the High King's domains.

In doing so has found a way of retaining his glorious title of The Special One. Wherever he goes, he will have the strength to inspire an army to battle for the Cup of Cups. In so doing he will remain a threat in the dreams of the High King.

Quizzes

Quiz 1

Q1: José's full name is

José Mario Santos Mourinho Félix

José di Maria Mourinho

José del Agua dos Santos Mourinho

Q2: He was born in a comfortable suburb of

Porto

Lisbon

Alicante

Q3: His father was

The owner of a factory making shipping accessories

A Portuguese football international

A school master and gifted football coach

Q4: He studied at a business school, leaving

After one day

At the end of the first week

After walking out of a final examination

Q5 One of his first coaching experiences was with

The Scottish Football Association

The Irish Football Association

The Newcastle United Football Club

Q6: On his appointment by Roman Abramovich for Chelsea for the first time

He was the owner's first choice

He was the owner's second choice after Sven-Göran Eriksson

He was the owner's second choice after Bobby Robson

Q7: According to the Guardian Newspaper, how did José reply publically to the question *why do you speak such good Italian*?

My wife taught me

I have to say honestly and without modesty that I have a gift for languages

I am not a dickhead

Q8: How do we know what Mourinho said to his playing staff on the pitch after losing to Liverpool in November 2015?

A newspaper hired a lip reader

A member of staff told a newspaper journalist

A member of staff told a player who told his agent

Q9: what was Mourinho believed to have said to his playing staff on the pitch after Chelsea lost to Liverpool in November 2015?

Your jobs are on the line. Six losses. It's unbelievable

You saw the ones who didn't play. It is always the same players

The problem was the ***, he didn't give *** the yellow card

Q10: what did Mourinho say publically after Real Madrid lost to Barcelona in the Champions' league semi-finals in April 2011

I did not hear anyone tell their players they should use the referee's changing room.

If I tell the referee and UEFA what I think, my career ends

We had more chances which is why I say we were the better team

Quiz 2

Q1: The name of José's influential agent for many years is

Jorge Mendes

Xavier Mendes

Jorge Valdano

Q2: One diminutive for Mourinho among his players is

Jambo

Jo

Mou

Q3: When Frank Rijkaard stepped down at Barcelona in 2008, the first choice of coach was Pep Guardiola over José Mourinho because

he had more experience as player and coach at the highest level

the political tensions between Barcelona and Real Madrid worked against José

he met more of their tick-list of factors

Q4: Before a match against Levante in 2010 Mourinho instructed his staff

To memorise details of Levante players' private lives to abuse them with

To motivate his players with promises of secret extra bonuses for every goal scored

To visit the pitch and measure the length of the grass

Q5: Which of these books was **not** written about José Mourinho?

The Portuguese man of War

The Special One

Mourinho: Anatomy of a winner

Q6: which book about José was reviewed by the distinguished political scientist David Runciman?

Mourinho: Anatomy of a winner

The Portuguese man of War

The Special One

Q7: What did José once do when Joe Cole scored a great goal for Chelsea?

Called him to the touchline and criticised him for showboating

Called him to touchline and kissed him

Ran to the corner flag and back to the dugout in celebration

Q8: When José was asked about his religious beliefs, in a press conference in 2007

He said his religion was personal and not a matter for a football conference

He ducked the question

He refused, saying he had met the Pope during his time in Italy who would not say what football team he supported either.

Q9: In December 2015, what did Sir Alex Ferguson tell Roman Abramovich about José?

It would be foolish to sack him

There was no better manager in Europe than José but no one is bigger than the team

José would leave unless he was given more say over player signings

Q10: In José's first season with Porto

He won the EUFA cup and finished second to Benfica in the league

He won the league but lost to Celtic in the EUFA cup

He won the treble

Quiz 3

Q1: In José's second season with Porto in 2003-4

He won the EUFA champions league and the EUFA super cup

His only trophy was the league title

He won the EUFA champions league

Q2: At the end of the 2003-4 Season he moved to Chelsea

after saying he wanted to go to Real Madrid

after saying he wanted to go to Manchester United

after saying he wanted to go to Liverpool

Q3: He became known as the Special One

On his arrival at Chelsea in 2004

After winning the Champions League cup with Porto

After arriving at Chelsea for the second time in 2013

Q4: During his stay at Chelsea starting in 2004 which statement is **not** true

His performance bonuses over three years were in excess of £22 million in total

He won six trophies for the club in three years

He was undefeated in all home games

Q5: He left Chelsea

For reasons that have never been published

'By mutual consent'

After failing to resolve a dispute between himself and owner Roman Abramovic over hiring Christiano Ronaldo

Q6: Where was his next managerial post after he first left Chelsea?

Inter Milan

Real Madrid

Barcelona

Q7: When he worked with Inter, which of these football giants did José **not** have a public dispute with?

Sir Bobby Charlton

Claudio Ranieri

Carlo Ancelotti

Q8: Which of these came true in 2010 for José?

Reached semi-finals of European Champions league with third different club

He hired a cordon bleu chef to improve his players' food experience

He introduced compulsory language lessons for players

Q9: Which other celebrity could have been named along with José in Q8

Louis van Gaal

Sir Alex Ferguson

Claudio Ranieri

Q10: what is a trivote

A defensive formation favoured by José when he managed Real Madrid

A FIFA arrangement which gives three votes to some executives on crucial issues

Basque term of derision for defensive formation favoured by José when he managed Real Madrid

Answers to the Quiz Questions

Quiz 1

Q1: José's full name is
José Mario Santos Mourinho Félix

Q2: He was born in a comfortable suburb of
Lisbon

Q3: His father was
A Portuguese football international

Q4: He studied at a business school, leaving
After one day

Q5 One of his first coaching experiences was with
The Scottish Football Association

Q6: On his appointment by Roman Abramovich for Chelsea for
the first time
He was the owner's first choice

Q7: According to the Guardian, how did José reply publically to
the question *why do you speak such good Italian*?
I am not a dickhead

Q8: How do we know what Mourinho said to his playing staff
on the pitch after losing to Liverpool in November 2015?
A newspaper hired a lip reader

Q9: what is Mourinho believed to have said to his playing staff
on the pitch after Chelsea lost to Liverpool in November 2015?
The problem was the ***, he didn't give *** the yellow card

Q10: what did Mourinho say publically after Real Madrid lost to
Barcelona in the Champions' league semi-finals in April 2011
If I tell the referee and UEFA what I think, my career ends

Quiz 2

Q1: The name of José's influential agent for many years is
Jorge Mendes

Q2: One diminutive for Mourinho among his players is
Mou

Q3: When Frank Rijkaard stepped down at Barcelona in 2008,
the first choice of coach was Pep Gaurdiola over José Mourinho
because
he met more of their tick-list of factors

Q4: Before a match against Levante in 2010 Mourinho
instructed his staff
To visit the pitch and measure the length of the grass

Q5: Which of these books was **not** written about José Mourinho
The Portuguese man of War

Q6: which book about José was reviewed by the distinguished
political scientist David Runciman?
Mourinho: Anatomy of a winner

Q7: What did José once do when Joe Cole scored a great goal
for Chelsea?
Called him to the touchline and criticised him for showboating

Q8: When asked about his religious beliefs, in a press
conference in 2007
He ducked the question

Q9: In December 2015, what did Sir Alex Ferguson tell Roman
Abramovic about José
It would be foolish to sack him

Q10: In José's first season with Porto
He won the treble

Quiz 3

Q1: In José's second season with Porto in 2003-4
He won the EUFA champions league

Q2: At the end of the 2003-4 Season he moved to Chelsea
after saying he wanted to go to Liverpool

Q3: He became known as the Special One
On his arrival at Chelsea in 2004

Q4: During his first stay at Chelsea starting in 2004 which
statement is **not** true
His performance bonuses were in excess of £22 million in total

Q5: He left Chelsea
'By mutual consent'

Q6: Where was his next managerial post after he first left
Chelsea?
Inter Milan

Q7: When he worked with Inter, which of these football giants
did José **not** have a public dispute with?
Sir Bobby Charlton

Q8: Which of these came true in 2010 for José?
Reached semi-finals of European Champions league with a third
different club
He hired a cordon bleu chef to improve his players' food
experience

Q9: Which other celebrity could have been named along with
José in Q8
Louis van Gaal

Q10: what is a trivote?
A defensive formation favoured by José when he managed Real
Madrid

Reference Sources

Preface
I recommend his History of Charisma as suitable:
http://www.palgrave.com/gb/book/9780230551534
My own students: http://www.amazon.co.uk/Dilemmas-
Leadership-Tudor-
Rickards/dp/1138814741/ref=dp_ob_image_bk

Introduction
first victory over José Mourinho in 14 clashes:
http://www.bbc.co.uk/sport/0/football/33667216
Chelsea suffered further losses:
http://www.bbc.co.uk/sport/0/football/34025310
written for leadership students:
https://leaderswedeserve.wordpress.com

Forward
a leader's charisma is based primarily on success:
https://leaderswedeserve.wordpress.com/2010/05/15/a-history-
of-charisma-book-review/

Early Days
Early days:
https://web.archive.org/web/20070331113408/http://www.newst
atesman.com:80/200512190026
When asked in a radio interview:
http://www.biographyonline.net/sport/football/José-
mourinho.html

Annus Mirabilis
John Dryden wrote a patriotic poem:
http://www.joh.cam.ac.uk/john-dryden-annus-mirabilis-1666
Porto pulls off the biggest surprise:
http://www.uefa.com/uefachampionsleague/season=2003/overvi
ew/index.html
A technical study:
http://www.zonalmarking.net/2010/03/08/teams-of-the-decade-
3-porto-2002-04/

principles of situational leadership:
https://leaderswedeserve.wordpress.com/2012/02/14/mick-mccarthy-sacked-the-case-examined-from-a-situational-leadership-perspective/
'it all depends':
http://thefutureofwork.net/leadership-it-all-depends-but-on-what/

Understanding José's Overnight Success
José had been immersed in a footballing culture:
https://web.archive.org/web/20070331113408/http://www.newstatesman.com:80/200512190026
Robson was an intuitive manager:
http://www.dailymail.co.uk/sport/football/article-1186928/Sir-Bobby-Robson-talks-local-hero-Steve-Harper-Newcastles-day-reckoning.html
particular his book Outliers:
http://cs.ecust.edu.cn/snwei/studypc/jsjdl/data/OutliersTheStoryOfSuccess.pdf
Mathew Syad in his book Bounce:
http://www.experttabletennis.com/bounce-by-matthew-syed/

The Tinkerman
He arrived in England in 2000 to coach Chelsea:
http://www.telegraph.co.uk/sport/football/competitions/premier-league/4771414/Ranieri-handed-the-Chelsea-hot-seat.html
In a short period of time, Ranieri produced results:
http://www.standard.co.uk/sport/football/carlo-cudicini-why-chelsea-fans-have-a-lot-to-thank-claudio-ranieri-for-a3136686.html
Then the most radical change in fortune:
http://news.bbc.co.uk/1/hi/business/3036838.stm
In his biography:
http://www.theguardian.com/sport/2008/mar/30/football.newsstory6

Chelsea's Magic Mystery Tour
had become the first team to win:
http://www.uefa.com/uefachampionsleague/season=1998/matches/round=1214/match=56379/postmatch/report/index.html

Chelsea defended the lead:
http://news.bbc.co.uk/sport1/hi/football/eng_prem/3553240.stm

Sweet Scent of Victory or Low-hanging Fruit?
It all went so well at first:
http://www.theguardian.com/football/2005/may/01/match.bolton
wanderers
Towards the start of the season:
https://www.buckinghamcovers.com/celebrities/view/317-José-
mourinho.php
astonishing defensive record:
http://www.dailymail.co.uk/sport/football/article-
2860448/Chelsea-unbeaten-flying-high-Premier-League.
Among the awards he won:
http://news.bbc.co.uk/sport1/hi/football/eng_prem/4478329.s
tm

Momentum Shifts
Boxing Day fixture against Reading:
https://leaderswedeserve.wordpress.com/2006/12/27/chelsea-
sets-a-question-of-momentum-in-sport/
Then the Boxing Day test:
http://news.bbc.co.uk/sport1/hi/cricket/england/6206590.stm

Paul Revere rides again (or "The Americans are coming")
The British are coming:
http://www.nationalcenter.org/PaulRevere%27sRide.html
It's Paul Revere in reverse:
http://leaderswedeserve.wordpress.com/2007/02/08/paul-revere-
rides-again/
footballing achievements of Chelsea and its billionaire owner:
http://leaderswedeserve.wordpress.com/2010/02/05/dilemmas-
of-leadership-idealism-versus-pragmatism-at-manchester-
united/]
'the two Davids':
http://www.dailymail.co.uk/sport/football/article-
2957678/Abuse-No-fans-value-good-owners-like-David-
Sullivan.html

What José did Next
Chelsea football club won a vital cup-game:
https://leaderswedeserve.wordpress.com/2007/03/07/what-José-did-next-how-a-leader-can-make-a-difference/

Trust me
An earlier post:
https://leaderswedeserve.wordpress.com/2007/04/21/mourhino%E2%80%99s-job-is-safe-you-can-trust-me/
proclaimed himself as a lifelong Manchester Unitedsupporter:
http://news.bbc.co.uk/sport1/hi/football/eng_prem/3091546.stm
tapping up' of a player contracted to another club:
http://www.telegraph.co.uk/sport/football/teams/chelsea/6199583/Chelseas-Peter-Kenyon-ups-and-downs.html
Fines were also imposed on José Mourinho and Ashley Cole although these were reduced on appeal:
http://news.bbc.co.uk/sport1/hi/football/eng_prem/4137124.stm
Peter Kenyon also quit:
http://www.telegraph.co.uk/sport/football/teams/chelsea/6197708/Peter-Kenyon-leaves-Chelsea.html

Destiny
José Mourinho leaves Chelsea football club:
https://leaderswedeserve.wordpress.com/2007/09/20/mourinho-fulfils-his-destiny/

Inter-Regnum
delivered the European Champions cup to Inter:
http://news.bbc.co.uk/sport1/hi/football/europe/8697017.stm
as the BBC report put it:
http://news.bbc.co.uk/sport1/hi/football/europe/8695530.stm

Why did José leave Inter?
an attitude which still prevails:
http://www.westbriton.co.uk/Chaos-fear-ensues-nature-ceases-behave/story-11503532-detail/story.html
Italy was preparing to play Germany:
http://web.archive.org/web/20060715141908/http://www.ft.com/cms/s/6129251e-0de3-11db-a385-0000779e2340.html

José's impact on Italian football:
http://www.dailymail.co.uk/sport/football/article-1253059/Its-José-Mourinho-versus-world-Italians-fed-Inter-Milan-manager-

Mourinho Tipped as next England Manager
https://leaderswedeserve.wordpress.com/2007/12/14/breaking-news-english-football-isolated-from-José-mourinho/

Fixture shift
https://leaderswedeserve.wordpress.com/2008/03/30/chelsea%E2%80%99s-fixture-shift-reveal%E2%80%99s-football%E2%80%99s-governance-problems/
Chelsea argues that the FA has put at risk:
http://www.independent.co.uk/sport/football/premier-league/fixture-switch-has-grant-up-in-arms-802376.html

Inverting the Pyramid
http://www.amazon.co.uk/Inverting-Pyramid-History-Football-Tactics/dp/1409102041/ref=sr_1_1?s=books&ie=UTF8&qid=1319530688&sr=1-1
another reference source: http://www.football-bible.com/soccer-info/football-formations.html

I remember, I remember
in a game to raise money for the 76-year-old's own cancer
charity: https://www.youtube.com/watch?v=B07BXA9LF1k
work of Robert Greanleaf: https://www.greenleaf.org/
BBC obituary:
http://news.bbc.co.uk/sport1/hi/football/4779033.stm
about a leader's moral compass and of authentic leadership:
http://www.billgeorge.org/page/true-north-discover-your-authentic-leadership

Mourinho Magic
José Mourinho brought his Inter Milan team to Old Trafford:
https://leaderswedeserve.wordpress.com/2009/03/12/no-mourinho-magic-in-manchester/

John Terry

https://leaderswedeserve.wordpress.com/2010/02/27/on-shaking-hands-and-creative-leadership-in-the-john-terry-wayne-bridges-saga/

Dreams and Obsessions
Barcelona are "obsessed" with winning the Champions League:
https://leaderswedeserve.wordpress.com/2010/04/28/José-dreams-and-pep-obsesses/

A History of Charisma: Book Review
https://leaderswedeserve.wordpress.com/2010/05/15/a-history-of-charisma-book-review/
Jay Conger and Rabindra Kanungo:
https://books.google.co.uk/books/about/Charismatic_Leadership_in_Organizations.html?id=dn8Y3QCqQPoC

Can we Learn from Brian Clough's Leadership Style?
https://leaderswedeserve.wordpress.com/2010/07/18/can-we-learn-much-from-brian-clough%E2%80%99s-leadership-style/

Real Rage
http://www.theguardian.com/football/2011/apr/28/José-mourinho-real-madrid-barcelona

José Mourinho: Cult leader and possessor of a mystic text
As the English researcher Alan Bryman noted:
http://www.ncsl.org.uk/media/F7B/97/randd-leaders-education-bryman.pdf
And later by Rickards and Clark:
http://cw.routledge.com/textbooks/0415355850/about/default.asp
http://www.worldsoccer.com/features/José-mourinho-60045
Mourinho was the FA's first choice:
http://www.theguardian.com/football/2007/dec/14/newsstory.sport15

Pat Riley, Alex Ferguson and José Mourinho
an invitation to speak at Harvard Business School:
http://hbr.org/2013/10/fergusons-formula/

Pat Riley of Miami Heat:
https://leaderswedeserve.wordpress.com/2011/07/24/%e2%80%9cpat-riley-and-sir-alex-ferguson-couldn%e2%80%99t-make-it-but-we-are-fortunate-to-have-with-us-tonight-instead%e2%80%a6%e2%80%9d.

Superhuman Powers
Mourinho reveals his superhuman powers:
https://leaderswedeserve.wordpress.com/2015/08/12/mourinho-reveals-his-superhuman-powers-of-diagnosing-medical-injuries-from-the-touch-line/

The Charismatic Reply
a typical charismatic response:
https://leaderswedeserve.wordpress.com/2015/09/19/the-charismatic-reply-José-responds-to-a-setback/
Against Everton, the evidence is clear:
http://www.bbc.co.uk/sport/0/football/34234100

Body Language after the Chelsea v Arsenal battle
a win at home over its great rivals Arsenal:
http://www.skysports.com/football/chelsea-vs-arsenal/341239
He seems to absorb or deny ambiguities:
http://www.bbc.co.uk/sport/0/football/34303523
Arsène Wenger interacts more:
http://www.bbc.co.uk/sport/0/football/34303951

The Battle with Klopp Begins
https://leaderswedeserve.wordpress.com/2015/10/11/has-mourinho-lost-the-charisma-battle-to-jurgen-klopp/

Man, Superman and Superwoman
https://leaderswedeserve.wordpress.com/2015/11/06/ronaldo-says-he-is-best-in-the-world-serena-says-she-is-superwoman-self-esteem-of-our-sporting-icons/

Prepare to Lose

https://leaderswedeserve.wordpress.com/2015/12/11/prepare-to-lose-astonishing-claims-about-José-mourinho-by-spanish-journalist/
It undermines Mourinho's claims:
http://www.dailymail.co.uk/sport/football/article-3354677/Chelsea-boss-José-Mourinho-understands-people-don-t-believe-him.html
A pure charismatic type:
https://bmackela.wordpress.com/author/bmackela/

José Mourinho has a long memory
I didn't have a Graeme Le Saux:
http://www.theguardian.com/football/2015/nov/23/José-mourinho-graeme-le-saux-israel-chelsea

Who's a Pretty Boy then?
not unaided by his sex appeal:
https://leaderswedeserve.wordpress.com/2015/12/07/whos-more-than-a-pretty-boy-then-the-case-of-justin-trudeau/
A thoughtful exploration in The Huffington Post:
http://www.huffingtonpost.ca/lauren-messervey/objectifying-trudeau-not-ok_b_8343342.html
explained to the Daily Telegraph:
http://www.telegraph.co.uk/news/science/science-news/8831399/Why-good-leaders-have-crooked-features.html
Harvard Business Review: https://hbr.org/2011/11/how-earlobes-can-signify-leadership-potential/ar/1

José Departs: Reflections on Perceptions versus Reality
For the second time: http://www.chelseafc.com/news/latest-news/2015/12/club-statement.html
The Daily Mail provided insights:
http://www.dailymail.co.uk/sport/football/article-3361549/José-Mourinho-stripped-away-Chelsea-players-self-esteem-lost-boss-isolated toxic-dressing-room.html

Annus Horribilis
This extended account serves as a summary of the news stories dealing with the last months of José Mourinho's second period

at Chelsea, July-December 2015. It also includes additional references accessed during the research.

This was all the sweeter for Arsenal Manager Arsène Wenger:
http://www.bbc.co.uk/sport/0/football/33667216
infuriated the wife of Chelsea Owner Roman Abramovich:
http://www.dailymail.co.uk/news/article-3199616/Women-united-Mrs-Abramovich-s-fury-Mourinho-outburst-against-female-doctor-ran-pitch-help-player.html
José's' disappointing record of misconduct':
http://www.telegraph.co.uk/sport/football/managers/José-mourinho/11980443/Chelsea-news-José-Mourinho-was-banned-for-refusing-to-leave-referees-room-and-issuing-foul-mouthed-rant.html
Mark Laurensen expresses hope:
http://www.bbc.co.uk/sport/0/football/34845747
Mourinho says current squad will 'fulfil trust' of owner:
http://www.bbc.co.uk/sport/0/football/34880037
'Only Tom Cruise could help Chelsea win title':
http://www.bbc.co.uk/sport/0/football/34891999
The latest player to fall out with the manager is Costa:
http://www.theguardian.com/football/2015/nov/29/chelsea-diego-costa-privileged-dropped-José-mourinho
http://www.telegraph.co.uk/sport/football/teams/chelsea/12024708/Chelsea-news-José-Mourinho-to-spend-week-assessing-Diego-Costas-state-of-mind.html
Kevin De Bruyne:
http://www.dailymail.co.uk/sport/football/article-3342580/Kevin-Bruyne-proving-José-Mourinho-wrong-Manchester-City-star-leading-contender-player-year.html
Liverpool's revival continues in 1-6 victory over Southampton. Klopp hailed as 'magician':
http://www.mirror.co.uk/sport/row-zed/jurgen-klopp-proves-hes-actual-6946756
Neville to Valencia, owner Lim keeps eye on Mou:
http://www.mirror.co.uk/sport/football/news/José-mourinho-touted-gary-nevilles-6945268

Man United PR Disaster:
http://www.dailymail.co.uk/news/article-503605/Man-Utds-Christmas-party-Booze-fights-sleaze-rape-allegation-tarnished-Britains-greatest-football-club.html
Mild Chelsea Partying:
http://www.standard.co.uk/sport/football/José-mourinho-my-chelsea-players-needed-to-party-it-s-good-for-team-morale-a3130156.html
Mourinho denies Valencia rumours:
http://www.independent.co.uk/sport/football/premier-league/diego-costa-exit-from-chelsea-speculation-leaves-José-mourinho-bemused-a6760421.html
Bournemouth defeat:
http://www.mirror.co.uk/sport/football/news/jimmy-floyd-hasselbaink-backed-chelsea-6970632
http://www.mirror.co.uk/sport/football/news/José-mourinho-only-remains-chelsea-6969880
December 9
http://www.mirror.co.uk/sport/football/news/José-mourinho-blasted-fake-who-6981285
Mourinho talks positively of Chelsea's chances of progressing:
http://www.skysports.com/football/news/11668/10094732/chelsea-2-0-porto-blues-raise-their-game-to-ease-the-pressure-on-José-mourinho
Expression of persecution?:
http://www.dailymail.co.uk/sport/football/article-3353521/José-Mourinho-stood-outside-dressing-room-half-time-avoid-ban-sending-Chelsea-team-late-second-half.html
John and José:
http://www.independent.co.uk/sport/football/has-it-turned-personal-between-José-mourinho-and-john-terry-at-chelsea-a6674441.html
Raniereri Sacked by Chelsea:
http://www.telegraph.co.uk/sport/2379979/Ranieri-is-sacked-by-Chelsea.html
Player revolt:

http://www.eurosport.com/football/premier-league/2015-2016/bbc-claim-unnamed-chelsea-star-would-rather-lose-than-win-for-mourinho_sto4974289/story.shtml
When, not if:http://www.dailymail.co.uk/sport/football/article-3361549/José-Mourinho-stripped-away-Chelsea-players-self-esteem-lost-boss-isolated-toxic-dressing-room.html

A helicopter hovers over a large brightly-lit building
The unfolding story was to dominate
sport:http://www.theguardian.com/football/live/2015/dec/17/Jos
é-mourinho-sacked-by-chelsea-live-updates

'Light Will Overcome Darkness'
a tradition broken only once:
http://royalcentral.co.uk/blogs/whatever-happened-to-the-1969-film-royal-family-5279
Today's message: http://www.dailymail.co.uk/news/article-3373701/Queen-uses-annual-Christmas-message-thank-people-bring-happiness-lives-including-families-confronts-darkness-hit-world-2015.html

The Magical Managerial Roundabout
Her set of voodoo dolls:
http://www.telegraph.co.uk/sport/football/managers/José-mourinho/12056721/Chelsea-sack-José-Mourinho-to-spark-momumental-levels-of-Twitter-trolling.html
Mourinho wanted to join Manchester United:
http://www.dailymail.co.uk/sport/football/article-3368202/José-Mourinho-ready-Manchester-United-job-former-Chelsea-boss-jump-chance-replace-Louis-van-Gaal.html
could either set the rest of the Premier League aflame:
http://www.telegraph.co.uk/sport/football/managers/José-mourinho/12059595/José-Mourinho-sees-Man-Utd-as-perfect-fit-but-fear-is-hell-either-set-rest-of-Premier-League-aflame...-or-just-United.html
a veteran general with an impressive list of battle honours:
http://www.espnfc.co.uk/bayern-munich/story/2762251/bayern-confirm-coach-carlo-ancelotti-will-succeed-guardiola

Zinedine Zidane, is an iconic footballer:
http://www.espnfc.co.uk/real-madrid/story/2784364/real-madrids-sacking-of-rafa-benitez-hard-to-understand;
http://www.bbc.co.uk/programmes/articles/lZPHgDdHzjS3Vsq
Gqhkkp6/what-s-zinedine-zidane-really-like?intc_type=promo&intc_location=sport&intc_campaign=zid
ane&intc_linkname=worldservice_fac_article1
to secure a Champions League place next season:
http://www.bbc.co.uk/sport/0/football/35218683
the Eva Careiro tribunal gets underway:
http://www.bbc.co.uk/sport/0/football/35241632
Chelsea approached Carlo Ancelotti:
http://www.dailymail.co.uk/sport/football/article-3389507/Chelsea-approached-Carlo-Ancelotti-five-weeks-sacking-José-Mourinho-Italian-rejected-Stamford-Bridge
http://www.mirror.co.uk/sport/football/news/chelsea-midfielder-oscar-plays-down-7137900
payments made to the club's players:
http://www.theguardian.com/football/2016/jan/08/chelsea-wage-bill-manchester-united-city?CMP=twt_gu
His theory of elites:
https://archive.org/stream/theoriesofsociet01pars#page/550/mod
e/2up
Future replacement for their Special One
http://www.mirror.co.uk/sport/football/news/chelsea-believe-diego-simeone-deal-7181815
straight out of the sacred text of José:
http://www.independent.co.uk/sport/football/premier-league/pep-guardiola-latest-says-he-could-delay-premier-league-move-to-arsenal-speculation-a6811261.html
He is planning a return to management:
http://www.thesun.co.uk/sol/homepage/sport/football/6866194/J
osé-Mourinho-Reddy-to-boss-Manchester-United.html

Index

Printed in Great Britain
by Amazon